TRANSLATIONS FROM
THE POETRY OF
Rainer Maria Rilke

RAINER MARIA RILKE

In Translations by M. D. HERTER NORTON
Letters to a Young Poet
Sonnets to Orpheus
Wartime Letters to Rainer Maria Rilke
Translations from the Poetry of Rainer Maria Rilke
The Lay of the Love and Death of Cornet Christopher Rilke
The Notebooks of Malte Laurids Brigge
Stories of God

Translated by STEPHEN SPENDER and J. B. LEISHMAN
Duino Elegies

Translated by JANE BANNARD GREENE and M. D. HERTER NORTON
Letters of Rainer Maria Rilke
Volume One, 1892–1910   Volume Two, 1910–1926

Translated by DAVID YOUNG
Duino Elegies

In Various Translations
Rilke on Love and Other Difficulties
Translations and Considerations of Rainer Maria Rilke
Compiled by JOHN J. L. MOOD

T: # TRANSLATIONS FROM THE POETRY OF

Rainer Maria Rilke

L Author

BY M. D. HERTER NORTON

W · W · NORTON & COMPANY

New York · London

W. W. Norton & Company, Inc., is the publisher of *The Norton Anthology of English Literature*, edited by M.H. Abrams *et al.*; *The Norton Anthology of Poetry*, edited by Alexander W. Allison *et al.*; *The Norton Anthology of American Literature*, edited by Nina Baym *et al.*; *The Norton Anthology of Short Fiction*, edited by R.V. Cassill; *The Norton Reader*, edited by Arthur M. Eastman *et al.*; *The Norton Anthology of Modern Poetry*, edited by Richard Ellmann and Robert O'Clair; *The Norton Anthology of Literature by Women*, edited by Sandra M. Gilbert and Susan Gubar; *The Norton Anthology of World Masterpieces*, edited by Maynard Mack *et al.*; and the Norton Critical Editions.

W. W. Norton & Company, Inc., 500 Fifth Avenue, New York, N.Y. 10110
W. W. Norton & Company Ltd., 37 Great Russell Street, London WC1B 3NU

ISBN 0-393-00156-3

831.912   567890

R457t

Contents

Contents

NEW POEMS (*NEUE GEDICHTE*)

From PART I (*Erster Teil*)

Foreword

"POEMS are, with the best knowledge and intention, not to be translated without losses. I always think one should stick to the originals." Surely no translator would disagree with this comment of Rilke's. Translators have a peculiar daring, in that they undertake to do to the best of their ability something they know cannot be done at all—not, that is, to ultimate reality. For identity can never be re-created; the poet speaks but once, and even the closest echo is already hollow with loss. Yet translation makes possible an approach to other cultures, other imaginings than our own, and the temptation to translate may become irresistible. Rilke himself not only yielded to it; he worked hard and joyfully at translating poetry from the Russian, English, French. In what follows I shall not be speaking, however, of what a poet may choose to do with his own re-creation of a poem from another language; of Rilke's rendering of the *Sonnets from the Portuguese,* for example, which in the process of translation become characteristic Rilke rather than a faithful German version of Elizabeth Barrett Browning's poems. I am concerned with translations that may be useful in offering acquaintance with the work of a great poet to those who cannot easily read him in his own tongue. It seems to me an essential part of such an undertaking to give the original text opposite the translation of each poem; the reader may then stick to it to whatever extent he is able, while those who know even very little German will be able to reconstruct the original for themselves, so that they too may to some extent repair the losses incurred in the change from one language to the other and from the poet's mind, via a translator's, to the reader's.

Literal translation seems to have been out of favor for poetry: perhaps because of certain difficulties, free interpretation has taken the place of the more direct transference of concepts from one language to the other that is more easily carried out in prose. Yet if the essence of a poem lies in the poetic idea; in the images and sensations, the symbols by which it is conveyed; in the color and sound, the quality of the words that are the instruments of those symbols; in the rhythms and the rhyme, the technical forms characteristic of the poet's expression; and, over and above these, in the spirit of the whole, which is more subtle and less definable than an analysis of its elements might imply— then all of these elements are, by nature of the poetic experience, more acutely concentrated than in prose and allow the translator fewer alternatives in approximating the original expression. They require, in short, finer tools, that the poetic idea may impinge upon the foreign understanding with some of the quality characteristic of poetry and of the particular poem in question. This means, I believe, that the translator of poetry must be still more exact than the translator of prose; more, not less, literal in resetting the symbols of a poem in his own language.

Since no two languages function exactly alike, it is obviously impossible to reproduce in the second or translator language all these elements exactly as they stand in the first or original language. But to resort for this reason to free interpretation, to depart entirely from the meaning of the first language at any convenient point in order to fit the poem into the second, does not really accomplish the purpose. For what becomes of a translation when the poet's characteristic symbols are altered?

Take the simple case of concrete description. Rilke, for example, is very accurate in his observation and recording of actualities. He describes the apostles, in the *Last Supper,* as "gathered around" Christ, for which one translator says that they "recline," later even alluding to "the couches." If Rilke mentions neither reclining nor couches, it is probably because in Leonardo's great picture, after seeing which he wrote the poem, there is no evidence of either: the apostles are far too agitated by the fateful moment. It happens that Goethe, praising Leonardo's wisdom in giving his subject a contemporary setting which makes use of details that would have been familiar to the Dominican monks themselves in the refectory below, comments on this very point with the words: "It would have been most inept in this place to stretch out the holy company on cushions (*Polster*)." But the translator of Rilke's poem need not even have been aware of the source of its inspiration; had he translated Rilke's words, he could not have failed to convey the truth of his picture.

I do not see what is gained by "interpreting" Rilke's conceptions— even the more abstract—in other terms than his own. Where he speaks in *The Carousel* of "the land that lingers [hesitates] long ere it goes under [goes down, sinks out of sight]," is it helpful to call this "the land that knows no want, whose distant end no childlike eyes discern"? Why even call the "white elephant" a "huge white elephant" when he gives us no indication that it is huge? Or where in *Childhood* he refers to images as *entgleitend,* i.e., slipping from or gliding from (presumably, by the context, from us, our grasp, perhaps the memory or the mind), does it give us any idea of Rilke's way of thinking to present them concretely and quite gratuitously as "seagulls wheeling"? And why drop two of these very images Rilke gives us in this same verse—of the sailboats that, being like his and more beautiful, cause the little boy to forget his own; and of his little face that "sinking shone out of the pond"—to substitute descriptive phrases cut from the translator's own whole cloth telling us the little boy had "and shoulders bare" as well as "and tousled hair"?

Small liberties these might seem, taken one by one, here and there, or if they did anything to make the translation more beautiful or true— but can the translator be truer than his model? One has only to read the English back into German to see how far they have taken him from his subject. Such alteration of the original symbols seems to me invariably to lead to the introduction of totally extraneous concepts, to additions and omissions that are entirely arbitrary, to paraphrasings that are less good by just so much as the measure of their departure from the original—in short, to a letting down in concentration of the poetic idea which in the end makes for poetry that is true neither to its model nor to itself.

One cannot help surmising that many of these departures from the original—if not most of them, indeed—are forced on the translator in his effort to preserve meter and, more particularly, rhyme. For word-values and qualities, as between German and English, it is, by and large and within the limits of idiom—note the qualification—not impossible to find satisfactory equivalents; that is translation's field, the game, the fun of translating. The handling of the more important elements of meter, as between the two languages, may offer occasional embarrassments but rarely any insurmountable difficulties; an irregular line that translates the words of the poet is surely more justifiable than a line stuffed with irrelevant words to fill out a given number of feet. But the rhyme-values of no two languages can possibly correspond (at least, I have never seen a translation in which they do), and from the way in which rhymes are for the most part negotiated in the translator language, it would seem that they must always do some violence to the original. Can anything but the desperate need of a rhyme have led one translator to allude to the apostles as "deranged" (it so conveniently agrees with "estranged")? Or induced another to make the little boy ride the lion "with quickened pant" (for the sake of that same "white elephant"), and the *Spanish Dancer* "leap higher" (rhymes with "fire"), though she is twirling her skirts in a dance specifically described as round, in which no leaping takes place? Perhaps it is also responsible for the "stealing" and the "feeling" that likewise crept without benefit of clergy into the stanza with the "shoulders bare" and "tousled hair."

To argue for keeping the closest possible parallels with the original and then make a plea for abandoning rhyme in the translation of rhymed verse, may seem scarcely logical. But rhyme, like meter, seems to me to belong to the more *technical* elements of form—if one may be allowed to make a division where in the poet's mind there may be none —whereas image, symbol, type of language, express the *intrinsic* qualities of the poetic idea. If either must be sacrificed to the other, is it not fairer to the poet's thought to keep the concept and let the rhyme go? We lose a lot when we lose rhyme: some of the succinctness and poignancy of form, in the lyric especially; certain effects of tempo, of cadence, though these may often be carried instead by meter and word-values; much of the color and play of words; the subtlety of internal rhyme. Yet drastic as this choice is, I have made it deliberately, believing that the original loses less in the end than when its images are perverted for the sake of a rhyme-scheme. If the reader is fairly given the meaning, he can get the rhyme-values by checking over the original text with the English. Such rhymes as turned up of their own accord I have not striven to eliminate; but I have, on the other hand, not used the little twists and subterfuges that sometimes make rhyme possible, having found them liable to misrepresent Rilke's style.

The principle of very close translation is naturally easier to follow out in some cases than in others. Yet I have found that almost always the best results, both in clarity of thought or image and in simplicity of expression, come with the closest idiomatic parallel. It goes without saying that certain German constructions cannot stand in English and that we have to free ourselves from them. Even so, one is easily trapped, in one's absorption with the German, into certain inversions that accord neither with English idiom nor with the natural prose sequence of modern poetry, whereas Rilke's style being straightforward and simple, the translator is liable to misrepresent it if he departs from the simple and straightforward idiom of his own language. To say that he simply has to do his best, in each case according to the context, might be taken to condone a lack of fidelity to the original. But it is only another way of saying that here he is obliged to depart from the letter in order to achieve the spirit. His only safe-guard, then, since depart he must, is to do so with images and terms that remain within recognizable reach of the poet's characteristic usage. His solution of such difficulties is up to his conscience on the one hand and his good taste on the other.

Perhaps a translation can never be more than the plaster cast of the original marble; at least, this literal method offers a way of recording, in a useful working model, what the poet is about. I am well aware that someone else working along similar lines might find happier parallels than mine. However one strives to keep both the letter and the spirit, one still remembers that the final grace, the final significance, are only to be found in the language of the poet himself.

I believe no such translations should be put forth without a thorough word-for-word overhauling by someone to whom the language of the original is native. Dictionaries have the peculiar failing that their German-English and English-German volumes often do not even agree with each other; but there are also shades of meaning and usage that one cannot properly expect to find in any dictionary. It has been my good fortune to have this essential help from two friends: from Frieda Planck Clarke, in many hours of devoted attention for which no formal acknowledgment can sufficiently express my gratitude, and from Hermann Weyl, of The Institute for Advanced Study at Princeton, who is a great lover of Rilke's poetry and to whom I am deeply indebted for his reading of many of the translations. I am no less indebted for arduous discussion and criticism of the English text to Philip Horton, who also knows his German and his Rilke well; and, for a reading of all but a few of these pages, to Edith Hamilton, whose own translations from the Greek, in addition to her knowledge of the German language, make her a keen and most understanding critic. I have learned much from these good friends in the course of this very exacting but very stimulating work, in which any errors or inadequacies are mine, not theirs.

Only after hesitating for many years did I begin experimenting with these literal translations of Rilke's poetry. If the selection of poems here included seems to suggest that spirit of experiment, I have tried, nevertheless, to make it representative of Rilke's work up to the long period of silence that fell after publication of the *Marienleben* and was not broken until the *Duineser Elegien* opened the last phase of his creative activity. Only a few of the *Erste Gedichte* are included, chosen at random from the many that might have served as well, to show how Rilke freed himself from the more conventional patterns of the German lyric which he was to develop so far beyond these early but characteristic beginnings. The longer romantic poems from the *Buch der Bilder* have been included because they also deal with typical material and have not to my knowledge been done into English; the same holds true of the group of poems called *Die Stimmen* (*The Voices*), which strongly reminds one of passages in the *Aufzeichnungen des Malte Laurids Brigge* (known here as *The Journal of My Other Self*). I would like to have included more of the *Neue Gedichte* than circumstances have allowed, but believe the examples that appear here give a clue to some of the beauties of that collection.

Rilke himself took great care in choosing the poems for his collections and placing them in satisfactory sequence, and while it is unfortunate that any selection inevitably disturbs this arrangement, I have found no valid reason for attempting to establish any other order than that in which the poems follow each other when drawn from the Insel-Verlag's standard edition of the *Collected Works*.

WILTON, CONNECTICUT,
for my mother's seventy-fifth birthday,
OCTOBER 18, 1938.

FIRST POEMS

FROM *Advent* (1898)

Das ist mein Streit:
Sehnsuchtgeweiht
durch alle Tage schweifen.
Dann, stark und breit,
mit tausend Wurzelstreifen
tief in das Leben greifen—
und durch das Leid
weit aus dem Leben reifen,
weit aus der Zeit!

This is my strife:
dedicate to desire
through all days to roam.
Then, strong and wide,
with a thousand root-fibers
deep into life to gripe—
and through pain
far beyond life to ripen,
far beyond time!

Du meine heilige Einsamkeit,
du bist so reich und rein und weit
wie ein erwachender Garten.
Meine heilige Einsamkeit du—
halte die goldenen Türen zu,
vor denen die wünsche warten.

Thou my sacred solitude,
thou art as rich and clean and wide
as an awakening garden.
My sacred solitude thou—
hold shut the golden doors
before which wishes wait.

Der Bach hat leise Melodien,
und fern ist Staub und Stadt;
die Wipfel winken her und hin
und machen mich so matt.

Der Wald ist wild, die Welt ist weit,
mein Herz ist hell und gross;
es hält die blasse Einsamkeit
mein Haupt in ihrem Schoss.

The brook has gentle melodies,
and far is dust and city;
the tree-tops are swaying to and fro
and making me so weary.

The wood is wild, the world is wide,
my heart is clear and big;
pale solitude is holding
my head upon her lap.

Ich liebe vergessene Flurmadonnen,
die ratlos warten auf irgendwen,
und Mädchen, die an einsamen Bronnen,
Blumen im Blondhaar, träumen gehn,

und Kinder die in die Sonne singen
und staunend gross zu den Sternen sehn,
und die Tage, wenn sie mir Lieder bringen,
und die Nächte, wenn sie in Blüten stehn.

I love forgotten field-madonnas
who wait for someone helplessly,
and girls who go by lonely springs,
flowers in their fair hair, to dream,

and children who sing in the sun and look
wondering wide-eyed to the stars,
and the days, when they bring me songs,
and the nights, when they stand in bloom.

Pfauenfeder:
in deiner Feinheit sondergleichen,
wie liebte ich dich schon als Kind.
Ich hielt dich für ein Liebeszeichen,
das sich an silberstillen Teichen
in kühler Nacht die Elfen reichen,
wenn alle Kinder schlafen sind.

Und weil Grossmütterchen, das gute,
mir oft von Wünschegerten las,
so träumte ich, du zartgemute,
in deinen feinen Fasern flute
die kluge Kraft der Rätselrute—
und suchte dich im Sommergras.

Peacockfeather:
peerless in your elegance,
how I loved you even as a child.
I took you for a love-token
which by silversilent ponds
elves in cool night hand each other,
when children all are gone to sleep.

And since good little Grandmama
often read me of wishing-wands,
I dreamed, you delicate of air,
there flowed in your fine filaments
the crafty force of the divining-rod—
and sought you in the summer grass.

Weisst du, ich will mich schleichen
leise aus lautem Kreis,
wenn ich erst die bleichen
Sterne über den Eichen
blühen weiss.

Wege will ich erkiesen,
die selten wer betritt
in blassen Abendwiesen—
und keinen Traum, als diesen:
Du gehst mit.

Do you know, I would quietly
slip from the loud circle,
when first I know the pale
stars above the oaks
are blooming.

Ways will I elect
that seldom any tread
in pale evening meadows—
and no dream but this:
You come too.

Mir war so weh. Ich sah dich blass und bang.
Das war im Traum. Und deine Seele klang.

Ganz leise tönte meine Seele mit,
und beide Seelen sangen sich: Ich litt.

Da wurde Friede tief in mir. Ich lag
im Silberhimmel zwischen Traum und Tag.

I grieved so much. I saw you pale and fearing.
That was in dream. And your soul rang.

All softly my soul sounded with it,
and both souls sang themselves: I suffered.

Then peace came deep in me. I lay
in the silver heaven between dream and day.

Weisst du, dass ich dir müde Rosen flechte
ins Haar, das leis ein weher Wind bewegt—
Siehst du den Mond, wie eine silberechte
Merkmünze, und ein Bild ist eingeprägt:
ein Weib, das lächelnd dunkle Dornen trägt—
Das ist das Zeichen toter Liebesnächte.

Fühlst du die Rosen auf der Stirne sterben?
Und jede lässt die Schwester schauernd los
und muss allein verdarben und verderben,
und alle fallen fahl in deinen Schoss.
Dort sind sie tot. Ihr Leid war leis und gross.
Komm in die Nacht. Und wir sind Rosenerben.

Do you know that I am winding weary roses
in your hair which soft a sad wind stirs—
Do you see the moon, like a pure silver
medal, and a likeness there engraved:
a woman, who smilingly bears dark thorns—
That is the sign of love-nights that are dead.

Do you feel the roses dying on your brow?
And each one shuddering lets its sister go
and alone must perish and decay,
and all are falling faded in your lap.
There they are dead. Their hurt was soft and great.
Come in the night. And we are roses' heirs.

Kannst du die alten Lieder noch spielen?
Spiele, Liebling. Sie wehn durch mein Weh
wie die Schiffe mit silbernen Kielen,
die nach heimlichen Inselzielen
treiben im leisen Abendsee.

Und sie landen am Blütengestade,
und der Frühling ist dort so jung.
Und da findet an einsamem Pfade
vergessene Götter in wartender Gnade
meine müde Erinnerung.

Can you still play the old songs?
Play, darling. They waft through my woe
like those ships with silver keels
that towards secret island havens
sail on the soft evening sea.

And they land by the flowering shore,
and the Spring there is so young.
And there on lonely pathways
forgotten gods in waiting grace
my weary remembrance finds.

※※ ※※

THE BOOK OF PICTURES

FROM *The First Book, Part 1*

※※ ※※

EINGANG

Wer du auch seist: am Abend tritt hinaus
aus deiner Stube, drin du alles weisst;
als letztes vor der Ferne liegt dein Haus:
Wer du auch seist.
Mit deinen Augen, welche müde kaum
von der verbrauchten Schwelle sich befrein,
hebst du ganz langsam einen schwarzen Baum
und stellst ihn vor den Himmel: schlank, allein.
Und hast die Welt gemacht. Und sie ist gross
und wie ein Wort, das noch im Schweigen reift.
Und wie dein Wille ihren Sinn begreift,
lassen sie deine Augen zärtlich los . . .

PRELUDE

Whoever you are: at evening step forth
out of your room, where all is known to you;
last thing before the distance lies your house:
whoever you are.
With your eyes, which wearily
scarce from the much-worn threshold free themselves,
you lift quite slowly a black tree
and place it against the sky: slender, alone.
And you have made the world. And it is large
and like a word that yet in silence ripens.
And as your will takes in the sense of it,
tenderly your eyes let it go . . .

AUS EINEM APRIL

Wieder duftet der Wald.
Es heben die schwebenden Lerchen
mit sich den Himmel empor, der unseren Schultern schwer war;
zwar sah man noch durch die Äste den Tag, wie er leer war,—
aber nach langen, regnenden Nachmittagen
kommen die goldübersonnten
neueren Stunden,
vor denen flüchtend, an fernen Häuserfronten
alle die wunden
Fenster furchtsam mit Flügeln schlagen.

Dann wird es still. Sogar der Regen geht leiser
über der Steine ruhig dunkelnden Glanz.
Alle Geräusche ducken sich ganz
in die glänzenden Knospen der Reiser.

FROM AN APRIL

Again the forest is fragrant.
The soaring larks lift up
aloft with them the sky that to our shoulders was heavy;
one still saw the day through the branches, indeed, that it was empty—
but after 'long, raining afternoons
come the gold-besunned
newer hours,
before which fleeing on far housefronts
all the wounded
windows fearfully beat with wings.

Then it grows still. Even the rain goes softer
over the quietly darkening glint of the stones.
All sounds duck entirely away
in the glistening buds of the brushwood.

MUSIK

Was spielst du, Knabe? Durch die Gärten gings
wie viele Schritte, flüsternde Befehle.
Was spielst du, Knabe? Siehe, deine Seele
verfing sich in den Stäben der Syrinx.

Was lockst du sie? Der Klang ist wie ein Kerker,
darin sie sich versäumt und sich versehnt;
stark ist dein Leben, doch dein Lied ist stärker,
an deine Sehnsucht schluchzend angelehnt.—

Gib ihr ein Schweigen, dass die Seele leise
heimkehre in das Flutende und Viele,
darin sie lebte, wachsend, weit und weise,
eh du sie zwangst in deine zarten Spiele.

Wie sie schon matter mit den Flügeln schlägt:
So wirst du, Träumer, ihren Flug vergeuden,
dass ihre Schwinge, vom Gesang zersägt,
sie nicht mehr über meine Mauern trägt,
wenn ich sie rufen werde zu den Freuden.

MUSIC

What are you playing, boy? Through the gardens it went
like many steps, like whispering commands.
What are you playing, boy? See, your soul
is entangled in the rods of the syrinx.

Why do you lure her? The sound is like a prison
where loitering and languishing she lies;
strong is your life, and yet your song is stronger,
against your longing leaning sobbingly.—

Give her a silence, that the soul may softly
turn home into the flooding and the fullness
in which she lived, growing, wide and wise,
ere you constrained her in your tender playings.

How she already wearier beats her wings:
Thus will you, dreamer, waste her flight away,
so that her pinions, sawn through by the singing,
no more may carry her across my walls
when I shall call her in to the delights.

DIE ENGEL

Sie haben alle müde Münde
und helle Seelen ohne Saum.
Und eine Sehnsucht (wie nach Sünde)
geht ihnen manchmal durch den Traum.

Fast gleichen sie einander alle;
in Gottes Gärten schweigen sie,
wie viele, viele Intervalle
in seiner Macht und Melodie.

Nur wenn sie ihre Flügel breiten,
sind sie die Wecker eines Winds:
Als ginge Gott mit seinen weiten
Bildhauerhänden durch die Seiten
im dunklen Buch des Anbeginns.

THE ANGELS

All of them have weary mouths
and bright souls without seam.
And a yearning (as toward sin)
goes sometimes through their dream.

Almost they are all alike;
in God's gardens they keep silent,
like many, many intervals
in his might and melody.

Only when they spread their wings
are they the wakers of a wind:
As though God went with his wide
sculptor-hands through the pages
in the dark book of first beginning.

KINDHEIT

Da rinnt der Schule lange Angst und Zeit
mit Warten hin, mit lauter dumpfen Dingen.
O Einsamkeit, o schweres Zeitverbringen . . .
Und dann hinaus: die Strassen sprühn und klingen,
und auf den Plätzen die Fontänen springen,
und in den Gärten wird die Welt so weit.—
Und durch das alles gehn im kleinen Kleid,
ganz anders als die andern gehn und gingen—:
O wunderliche Zeit, o Zeitverbringen,
o Einsamkeit.

Und in das alles fern hinauszuschauen:
Männer und Frauen; Männer, Männer, Frauen
und Kinder, welche anders sind und bunt;
und da ein Haus und dann und wann ein Hund
und Schrecken lautlos wechselnd mit Vertrauen—:
O Trauer ohne Sinn, o Traum, o Grauen,
o Tiefe ohne Grund.

Und so zu spielen: Ball und Ring und Reifen
in einem Garten, welcher sanft verblasst,
und manchmal die Erwachsenen zu streifen,
blind und verwildert in des Haschens Hast,
aber am Abend still, mit kleinen steifen
Schritten nach Haus zu gehn, fest angefasst—:

CHILDHOOD

The long anxiety and time of school
runs on with waiting, with nothing but dull things.
O solitude, o heavy spending of time . . .
Then out: the streets are ringing and asparkle,
and in the squares the fountains leaping,
and in the gardens the world becomes so wide.—
And to go through it all in one's small suit,
quite differently than others go and used to go—:
O wonderful strange time, o spending of time,
o solitude.

And to look out far away into it all:
men and women; men, men, women
and children who are different and gay-colored;
and there a house and now and then a dog
and terror changing soundlessly to trust—:
O sorrow without meaning, o dream, o dread,
o groundless deep.

And so to play: ball and ring and hoop
in a garden that is gently paling,
and sometimes to brush against the grown-ups,
blind and dishevelled in the haste of tag,
but in the evening quietly, with small stiff
steps to go walking home, firmly held on to—:

O immer mehr entweichendes Begreifen,
o Angst, o Last.

Und stundenlang am grossen grauen Teiche
mit einem kleinen Segelschiff zu knien;
es zu vergessen, weil noch andre gleiche
und schönere Segel durch die Ringe ziehn,
und denken müssen an das kleine bleiche
Gesicht, das sinkend aus dem Teiche schien—:
O Kindheit, o entgleitende Vergleiche.
Wohin? Wohin?

O ever more elusive understanding,
o fear, o burden.

And for hours on end beside the big gray pond
to kneel with a little sailing-boat;
to forget it because still other sails
like it and finer are drawing through the circles,
and to have to think of that small pale
face that sinking shone out of the pond—:
O childhood, o images slipping from us.
Whither? Whither?

AUS EINER KINDHEIT

Das Dunkeln war wie Reichtum in dem Raume,
darin der Knabe, sehr verheimlicht, sass.
Und als die Mutter eintrat wie im Traume,
erzitterte im stillen Schrank ein Glas.
Sie fühlte, wie das Zimmer sie verriet,
und küsste ihren Knaben: Bist du hier? . . .
Dann schauten beide bang nach dem Klavier,
denn manchen Abend hatte sie ein Lied,
darin das Kind sich seltsam tief verfing.

Er sass sehr still. Sein grosses Schauen hing
an ihrer Hand, die ganz gebeugt vom Ringe,
als ob sie schwer in Schneewehn ginge,
über die weissen Tasten ging.

FROM A CHILDHOOD

The darkening was like riches in the room
in which the boy, withdrawn and secret, sat.
And when his mother entered as in a dream,
a glass quivered in the silent cabinet.
She felt how the room had given her away,
and kissed her boy: Are you here? . . .
Then both gazed timidly towards the piano,
for many an evening she would play a song
in which the child was strangely deeply caught.

He sat quite still. His big gaze hung
upon her hand which, all bowed down by the ring,
as it were heavily in snowdrifts going,
over the white keys went.

DER KNABE

Ich möchte einer werden so wie die,
die durch die Nacht mit wilden Pferden fahren,
mit Fackeln, die gleich aufgegangenen Haaren
in ihres Jagens grossem Winde wehn.
Vorn möcht ich stehen wie in einem Kahne,
gross und wie eine Fahne aufgerollt.
Dunkel, aber mit einem Helm von Gold,
der unruhig glänzt. Und hinter mir gereiht
zehn Männer aus derselben Dunkelheit
mit Helmen, die wie meiner unstet sind,
bald klar wie Glas, bald dunkel, alt und blind.
Und einer steht bei mir und bläst uns Raum
mit der Trompete, welche blitzt und schreit,
und bläst uns eine schwarze Einsamkeit,
durch die wir rasen wie ein rascher Traum:
die Häuser fallen hinter uns ins Knie,
die Gassen biegen sich uns schief entgegen,
die Plätze weichen aus: wir fassen sie,
und unsere Rosse rauschen wie ein Regen.

THE BOY

I want to become like one of those
who through the night go driving with wild horses,
with torches that like loosened hair
blow in the great wind of their chasing.
Forward I want to stand as in a skiff,
large and like a flag unfurled.
Dark, but with a helm of gold that glints
uneasily. And in a row behind me
ten men out of the selfsame darkness
with helmets that are as unstaid as mine,
now clear as glass, now dark and old and blind.
And one beside me stands and blasts us space
upon his trumpet that flashes and that screams,
and blasts us a black solitude
through which we tear like a rapid dream:
the houses fall behind us to their knees,
the streets bend slantingly to meet us,
the squares give way: we take hold of them,
with our horses rushing like a rain.

DAS ABENDMAHL

Sie sind versammelt, staunende Verstörte,
um ihn, der wie ein Weiser sich beschliesst,
und der sich fortnimmt denen er gehörte,
und der an ihnen fremd vorüberfliesst.
Die alte Einsamkeit kommt über ihn,
die ihn erzog zu seinem tiefen Handeln;
nun wird er wieder durch den Ölwald wandeln,
und die ihn lieben, werden vor ihm fliehn.

Er hat sie zu dem letzten Tisch entboten
und (wie ein Schuss die Vögel aus den Schoten
scheucht) scheucht er ihre Hände aus den Broten
mit seinem Wort: sie fliegen zu ihm her;
sie flattern bange durch die Tafelrunde
und suchen einen Ausgang. Aber er
ist überall wie eine Dämmerstunde.

THE LAST SUPPER

They are gathered, astounded and disturbed,
round him who, like a sage resolved to his end,
takes himself away from those he belonged to,
and who alien past them flows.
The old loneliness comes over him
that reared him to the doing of his deep acts;
now again will he wander through the olive grove,
and those who love him will take flight before him.

He has summoned them to the last supper
and (as a shot scatters birds out of the sheaves)
he scatters their hands from among the loaves
with his word: they fly across to him;
they flutter anxious through the table's round
and try to find a way out. But he
is everywhere like a twilight-hour.

THE BOOK OF PICTURES

FROM *The First Book, Part II*

INITIALE

Aus unendlichen Sehnsüchten steigen
endliche Taten wie schwache Fontänen,
die sich zeitig und zitternd neigen.
Aber, die sich uns sonst verschweigen,
unsere fröhlichen Kräfte—zeigen
sich in diesen tanzenden Tränen.

INITIAL

Out of infinite yearnings rise
finite deeds like feeble fountains,
that early and trembling droop.
But those, else silent within us,
our happy strengths—reveal themselves
in these dancing tears.

ZUM EINSCHLAFEN ZU SAGEN

Ich möchte jemanden einsingen,
bei jemandem sitzen und sein.
Ich möchte dich wiegen und kleinsingen
und begleiten schlafaus und schlafein.
Ich möchte der einzige sein im Haus,
der wüsste: Die Nacht war kalt.
Und möchte horchen herein und hinaus
in dich, in die Welt, in den Wald.—
Die Uhren rufen sich schlagend an,
und man sieht der Zeit auf den Grund.
Und unten geht noch ein fremder Mann
und stört einen fremden Hund.
Dahinter wird Stille. Ich habe gross
die Augen auf dich gelegt;
sie halten dich sanft und lassen dich los,
wenn ein Ding sich im Dunkel bewegt.

TO SAY FOR GOING TO SLEEP

I would like to sing someone to sleep,
by someone to sit and be.
I would like to rock you and croon you to sleep
and attend you in slumber and out.
I would like to be the only one in the house
who would know: The night was cold.
And would like to hearken within and without
to you, to the world, to the wood.—
The clocks call striking to each other,
and one sees to the bottom of time.
And below a strange man passes yet
and rouses a strange dog.
Behind that comes stillness. I have laid
my eyes upon you wide;
they hold you gently and let you go
when some thing stirs in the dark.

MENSCHEN BEI NACHT

Die Nächte sind nicht für die Menge gemacht.
Von deinem Nachbar trennt dich die Nacht,
und du sollst ihn nicht suchen trotzdem.
Und machst du nachts deine Stube licht,
um Menschen zu schauen ins Angesicht,
so musst du bedenken: wem.

Die Menschen sind furchtbar vom Licht entstellt,
das von ihren Gesichtern träuft,
und haben sie nachts sich zusammengesellt,
so schaust du eine wankende Welt
durcheinandergehäuft.
Auf ihren Stirnen hat gelber Schein
alle Gedanken verdrängt,
in ihren Blicken flackert der Wein,
an ihren Händen hängt
die schwere Gebärde, mit der sie sich
bei ihren Gesprächen verstehn;
und dabei sagen sie: Ich und Ich
und meinen: Irgendwen.

PEOPLE BY NIGHT

The nights are not made for the multitude.
From your neighbor the night divides you,
and you shall not seek him despite it.
And if at night you light your room
to look people in the face,
then you must consider: whom.

People are fearfully disfigured by the light
that drips from their countenances,
and if at night they have foregathered,
you look on a wavering world
all heaped together.
Upon their foreheads yellow shine
has driven away all thoughts,
in their glances flickers the wine,
on their hands hangs
the heavy gesture with which in their talks
they understand each other;
and withal they say: I and I
and mean: Anybody.

DER NACHBAR

Fremde Geige, gehst du mir nach?
In wieviel fernen Städten schon sprach
deine einsame Nacht zu meiner?
Spielen dich Hunderte? Spielt dich einer?

Gibt es in allen grossen Städten
solche, die sich ohne dich
schon in den Flüssen verloren hätten?
Und warum trifft es immer mich?

Warum bin ich immer der Nachbar derer,
die dich bange zwingen zu singen
und zu sagen: Das Leben ist schwerer
als die Schwere von allen Dingen?

THE NEIGHBOR

Strange violin, are you following me?
In how many distant cities already
has your lonely night spoken to mine?
Do hundreds play you? Or does one?

Are there in all great cities
such as without you would
already have lost themselves in the rivers?
And why does it always happen to me?

Why am I always neighbor to those
who fearfully force you to sing
and to say: Life is heavier
than the heaviness of all things?

BANGNIS

Im welken Walde ist ein Vogelruf,
der sinnlos scheint in diesem welken Walde.
Und dennoch ruht der runde Vogelruf
in dieser Weile, die ihn schuf,
breit wie ein Himmel auf dem welken Walde.
Gefügig räumt sich alles in den Schrei.
Das ganze Land scheint lautlos drin zu liegen,
der grosse Wind scheint sich hineinzuschmiegen,
und die Minute, welche weiter will,
ist bleich und still, als ob sie Dinge wüsste,
an denen jeder sterben müsste,
aus ihm herausgestiegen.

APPREHENSION

There is a bird-call in the withered wood
that in this withered wood seems meaningless.
And even so the rounded bird-call rests
in this while that shaped it,
wide as a sky upon the withered wood.
Easily all things range themselves in the cry.
The whole land seems soundless to lie in it,
the great wind seems to nestle into it,
and the minute, wanting to go on,
has, pale and still, as though it knew things
of which anyone would have to die,
risen out of it.

KLAGE

O wie ist alles fern
und lange vergangen.
Ich glaube, der Stern
von welchem ich Glanz empfange,
ist seit Jahrtausenden tot.
Ich glaube, im Boot,
das vorüberfuhr,
hörte ich etwas Banges sagen.
Im Hause hat eine Uhr
geschlagen . . .
In welchem Haus? . . .
Ich möchte aus meinem Herzen hinaus
unter den grossen Himmel treten.
Ich möchte beten.
Und einer von allen Sternen
müsste wirklich noch sein.
Ich glaube, ich wüsste,
welcher allein
gedauert hat,
welcher wie eine weisse Stadt
am Ende des Strahls in den Himmeln steht . . .

LAMENT

O how are all things far
and long gone by!
I believe the star
from which I get radiance
has been dead for thousands of years.
I believe, in the boat
that passed over,
I heard something fearful said.
In the house a clock
struck . . .
In what house? . . .
I would like to step forth out of my heart
under the great sky.
I would like to pray.
And one of all the stars
must really still be.
I believe I would know
which one alone
has endured,
which one like a white city
stands at the end of the beam in the heavens . . .

HERBSTTAG

Herr: es ist Zeit. Der Sommer war sehr gross.
Leg deinen Schatten auf die Sonnenuhren,
und auf den Fluren lass die Winde los.

Befiehl den letzten Früchten voll zu sein;
gib ihnen noch zwei südlichere Tage,
dränge sie zur Vollendung hin und jage
die letzte Süsse in den schweren Wein.

Wer jetzt kein Haus hat, baut sich keines mehr.
Wer jetzt allein ist, wird es lange bleiben,
wird wachen, lesen, lange Briefe schreiben
und wird in den Alleen hin und her
unruhig wandern, wenn die Blätter treiben.

AUTUMN DAY

Lord, it is time. The summer was very big.
Lay thy shadow on the sundials,
and on the meadows let the winds go loose.

Command the last fruits that they shall be full;
give them another two more southerly days,
press them on to fulfillment and drive
the last sweetness into the heavy wine.

Who has no house now, will build him one no more.
Who is alone now, long will so remain,
will wake, read, write long letters
and will in the avenues to and fro
restlessly wander, when the leaves are blowing.

ERINNERUNG

Und du wartest, erwartest das Eine
das dein Leben unendlich vermehrt;
das Mächtige, Ungemeine,
das Erwachen der Steine,
Tiefen, dir zugekehrt.

Es dämmern im Bücherständer
die Bände in Gold und Braun;
und du denkst an durchfahrene Länder,
an Bilder, an die Gewänder
wiederverlorener Fraun.

Und da weisst du auf einmal: Das war es.
Du erhebst dich, und vor dir steht
eines vergangenen Jahres
Angst und Gestalt und Gebet.

REMEMBERING

And you wait, are awaiting the one thing
that will infinitely increase your life;
the powerful, the uncommon,
the awakening of stones,
depths turned towards you.

Dimly there gleam in the bookcase
the volumes in gold and brown;
and you think of lands journeyed through,
of pictures, of the apparel
of women lost again.

And you know all at once: That was it.
You arise, and before you stands
a bygone year's
anguish and form and prayer.

HERBST

Die Blätter fallen, fallen wie von weit,
als welkten in den Himmeln ferne Gärten;
sie fallen mit verneinender Gebärde.

Und in den Nächten fällt die schwere Erde
aus allen Sternen in die Einsamkeit.

Wir alle fallen. Diese Hand da fällt.
Und sieh dir andre an: es ist in allen.

Und doch ist Einer, welcher dieses Fallen
unendlich sanft in seinen Händen hält.

AUTUMN

The leaves are falling, falling as from way off,
as though far gardens withered in the skies;
they are falling with denying gestures.

And in the nights the heavy earth is falling
from all the stars down into loneliness.

We all are falling. This hand falls.
And look at others: it is in them all.

And yet there is one who holds this falling
endlessly gently in his hands.

AM RANDE DER NACHT

Meine Stube und diese Weite,
wach über nachtendem Land,—
ist Eines. Ich bin eine Saite,
über rauschende breite
Resonanzen gespannt.

Die Dinge sind Geigenleiber,
von murrendem Dunkel voll;
drin träumt das Weinen der Weiber,
drin rührt sich im Schlafe der Groll
ganzer Geschlechter . . .
Ich soll
silbern erzittern: dann wird
alles unter mir beben,
und was in den Dingen irrt,
wird nach dem Lichte streben,
das von meinem tanzenden Tone,
um welchen der Himmel wellt,
durch schmale, schmachtende Spalten
in die alten
Abgründe ohne
Ende fällt . . .

ON THE VERGE OF NIGHT

My room and this expanse,
awake over night-darkening land—
is one. I am a string,
across turbulent broad
resonances spanned.

Things are violin-bodies,
with muttering darkness full;
therein dreams the weeping of women,
therein stirs in its sleep the grumbling
of whole generations . . .
I must
silvernly vibrate: then will
everything under me quiver,
and what wanders lost in things
will strive towards the light
that from my dancing tone,
around which heaven throbs,
through narrow, craving rifts
into the old
abysses without
end falls . . .

VORGEFÜHL

Ich bin wie eine Fahne von Fernen umgeben.
Ich ahne die Winde, die kommen, ich muss sie leben,
während die Dinge unten sich noch nicht rühren:
die Türen schliessen noch sanft, und in den Kaminen ist Stille;
die Fenster zittern noch nicht, und der Staub ist noch schwer.

Da weiss ich die Stürme schon und bin erregt wie das Meer.
Und breite mich aus und falle in mich hinein
und werfe mich ab und bin ganz allein
in dem grossen Sturm.

PRESENTIMENT

I am like a flag by far spaces surrounded.
I sense the winds that are coming, I must live them
while things down below are not yet moving:
the doors are still shutting gently, and in the chimneys is silence;
the windows are not yet trembling, and the dust is still heavy.

Then already I know the storms and am stirred like the sea.
And spread myself out and fall back into myself
and fling myself off and am all alone
in the great storm.

ABEND

Der Abend wechselt langsam die Gewänder,
die ihm ein Rand von alten Bäumen hält;
du schaust: und von dir scheiden sich die Länder,
ein himmelfahrendes und eins, das fällt;

und lassen dich, zu keinem ganz gehörend,
nicht ganz so dunkel wie das Haus, das schweigt,
nicht ganz so sicher Ewiges beschwörend
wie das, was Stern wird jede Nacht und steigt;

und lassen dich (unsäglich zu entwirrn)
dein Leben, bang und riesenhaft und reifend,
so dass es, bald begrenzt und bald begreifend,
abwechselnd Stein in dir wird und Gestirn.

EVENING

The evening slowly changes the attire
held for it by a border of old trees;
you watch: and the lands part company with **you,**
one heavenward-ascending, one that falls;

and leave you, to neither quite belonging,
not quite so dark as the house that is silent,
not quite so surely conjuring the eternal
as that which turns to star each night and rises;

and leave you (inexpressibly to disentangle)
your life, fearing, gigantic, ripening, that it
becomes, now circumscribed, now comprehending,
alternately stone in you and star.

ERNSTE STUNDE

Wer jetzt weint irgendwo in der Welt,
ohne Grund weint in der Welt,
weint über mich.

Wer jetzt lacht irgendwo in der Nacht,
ohne Grund lacht in der Nacht,
lacht mich aus.

Wer jetzt geht irgendwo in der Welt,
ohne Grund geht in der Welt,
geht zu mir.

Wer jetzt stirbt irgendwo in der Welt,
ohne Grund stirbt in der Welt,
sieht mich an.

GRAVE HOUR

Who now weeps anywhere in the world,
without cause weeps in the world,
weeps over me.

Who now laughs anywhere in the night,
without cause laughs in the night,
laughs at me.

Who now moves anywhere in the world,
without cause moves in the world,
moves towards me.

Who now dies anywhere in the world,
without cause dies in the world,
looks at me.

STROPHEN

Ist einer, der nimmt alle in die Hand,
dass sie wie Sand durch seine Finger rinnen.
Er wählt die schönsten aus den Königinnen
und lässt sie sich in weissen Marmor hauen,
still liegend in des Mantels Melodie;
und legt die Könige zu ihren Frauen,
gebildet aus dem gleichen Stein wie sie.

Ist einer, der nimmt alle in die Hand,
dass sie wie schlechte Klingen sind und brechen.
Er ist kein Fremder, denn er wohnt im Blut,
das unser Leben ist und rauscht und ruht.
Ich kann nicht glauben, dass er unrecht tut;
doch hör ich viele Böses von ihm sprechen.

STROPHES

There's one who takes all people in his hand,
that they like sand between his fingers run.
He chooses the most lovely of the queens
and in white marble has them hewn for him,
still-lying in their mantel's melody;
and puts the kings to lie beside their wives,
fashioned out of the same stone as they.

There's one who takes all people in his hand,
that they are like faulty blades and break.
He is no stranger, for he lives in the blood
that is our life and stirs through us and rests.
I can't believe that he is doing wrong;
yet I hear many speaking evil of him.

THE BOOK OF PICTURES

FROM *The Second Book, Part I*

INITIALE

Gib deine Schönheit immer hin
ohne rechnen und reden.
Du schweigst. Sie sagt für dich: Ich bin.
Und kommt in tausendfachem Sinn,
kommt endlich über jeden.

INITIAL

Simply give away your beauty
without talk and reckoning.
You are still. She says for you: I am.
And comes in meaning thousandfold,
at last comes over everyone.

VERKÜNDIGUNG

DIE WORTE DES ENGELS

Du bist nicht näher an Gott als wir;
wir sind ihm alle weit.
Aber wunderbar sind dir
die Hände benedeit.
So reifen sie bei keiner Frau,
so schimmernd aus dem Saum:
Ich bin der Tag, ich bin der Tau,
du aber bist der Baum.

Ich bin jetzt matt, mein Weg war weit,
vergib mir, ich vergass,
was er, der gross in Goldgeschmeid
wie in der Sonne sass,
dir künden liess, du Sinnende,
(verwirrt hat mich der Raum).
Sieh: Ich bin das Beginnende,
du aber bist der Baum.

Ich spannte meine Schwingen aus
und wurde seltsam weit;
jetzt überfliesst dein kleines Haus
von meinem grossen Kleid.
Und dennoch bist du so allein
wie nie und schaust mich kaum;

ANNUNCIATION

THE WORDS OF THE ANGEL

Thou art not nearer to God than we;
we all are far from him.
Wonderfully nonetheless
are thy hands blessed.
No other woman's ripen so,
shimmering out so from the hem:
I am the day, I am the dew,
but thou art the tree.

I am weary now, my way was far,
forgive me, I forgot
what he, who great in gold adornment
sat as in the sun,
would have thee know, thou musing one,
(space has bewildered me).
See: I am what is beginning,
but thou art the tree.

I spread my wings out and became
wonderfully wide;
now thy small house overflows
with my great dress.
And still thou art alone as never
and scarcely seeest me;

das macht: Ich bin ein Hauch im Hain,
du aber bist der Baum.

Die Engel alle bangen so,
lassen einander los:
noch nie war das Verlangen so,
so ungewiss und gross.
Vielleicht, dass etwas bald geschieht,
das du im Traum begreifst.
Gegrüsst sei, meine Seele sieht:
du bist bereit und reifst.
Du bist ein grosses, hohes Tor,
und aufgehn wirst du bald.
Du meines Liedes liebstes Ohr,
jetzt fühle ich: Mein Wort verlor
sich in dir wie im Wald.

So kam ich und vollendete
dir tausendeinen Traum.
Gott sah mich an: er blendete . . .

Du aber bist der Baum.

because I am a breath in the grove,
but thou art the tree.

The angels all are so full of fear,
let go of one another:
never yet has longing been like this,
so undefined and great.
Perhaps something will happen soon
that thou in thy dream understandest.
Hail to thee, my soul beholds
thou art prepared and ripenest.
Thou art a gateway great and high
and thou shalt open soon.
Thou, my song's dearest ear,
now I feel: my word was lost
in thee as in a wood.

So I came and fulfilled for thee
a thousand and one dreams.
God looked at me: he dazzled . . .

But thou art the tree.

IN DER CERTOSA

Ein jeder aus der weissen Bruderschaft
vertraut sich pflanzend seinem kleinen Garten.
Auf jedem Beete steht, wer jeder sei.
Und einer harrt in heimlichen Hoffarten,
dass ihm im Mai
die ungestümen Blüten offenbarten
ein Bild von seiner unterdrückten Kraft.

Und seine Hände halten, wie erschlafft,
sein braunes Haupt, das schwer ist von den Säften,
die ungeduldig durch das Dunkel rollen,
und sein Gewand, das faltig, voll und wollen,
zu seinen Füssen fliesst, ist stramm gestrafft
um seinen Armen, die, gleich starken Schäften,
die Hände tragen, welche träumen sollen.

Kein Miserere und kein Kyrie
will seine junge runde Stimme ziehn,
vor keinem Fluche will sie fliehn;
sie ist kein Reh.
Sie ist ein Ross und bäumt sich im Gebiss,
und über Hürde, Hang und Hindernis
will sie ihn tragen weit und weggewiss,
ganz ohne Sattel will sie tragen ihn.

Er aber sitzt, und unter den Gedanken
zerbrechen fast die breiten Handgelenke,

IN THE CERTOSA

Each one of the white brotherhood,
planting, confides in his little garden.
Upon each bed stands noted who each is.
And one of them waits in secret pride ambitious
that in May
the impetuous blossoms should make manifest
to him a picture of his stifled strength.

And his hands, as though of tension slacked,
hold his brown head, heavy with the saps
that through the dark impatiently go rolling,
and his robe, in folds, full and woolen,
flowing to his feet, is stretched taut
about his arms, which, like strong shafts,
are carrying those hands that have to dream.

No Miserere and no Kyrie
would his round young voice draw forth,
nor flee before a curse;
it is no deer.
It is a steed and rears against the bit
and over hurdle, hill and hindrance it
would bear him far and certain of the way,
even without a saddle would it bear him.

But he sits, and underneath his thoughts
his broad wrists almost break, so heavy his

so schwer wird ihm der Sinn und immer schwerer.
Der Abend kommt, der sanfte Wiederkehrer,
ein Wind beginnt, die Wege werden leerer,
und Schatten sammeln sich im Talgesenke.
Und wie ein Kahn, der an der Kette schwankt,
so wird der Garten ungewiss und hangt
wie windgewiegt auf lauter Dämmerung.
Wer löst ihn los? . . .

Der Frate ist so jung,
und langelang ist seine Mutter tot.
Er weiss von ihr: sie nannten sie La Stanca;
sie war ein Glas, ganz zart und klar. Man bot
es einem, der es nach dem Trunk zerschlug
wie einen Krug.

So ist der Vater.
Und er hat sein Brot
als Meister in den roten Marmorbrüchen.
Und jede Wöchnerin in Pietrabianca
hat Furcht, das er des Nachts mit seinen Flüchen
vorbei an ihrem Fenster kommt und droht.

Sein Sohn, den er der Donna Dolorosa
geweiht in einer Stunde wilder Not,
sinnt im Arkadenhofe der Certosa,
sinnt, wie umrauscht von rötlichen Gerüchen:
denn seine Blumen blühen alle rot.

reflection grows and always heavier.
The evening comes, the gentle one returning,
a wind begins, the ways grow emptier,
and shadows gather in the valley's dip.
And like a boat that swings upon its chain,
so the garden is growing indistinct
and hangs as if wind-cradled on sheer twilight.
Who will release it? . . .

The frate is so young,
and full long his mother has been dead.
He knows about her: they called her La Stanca;
she was a glass, all delicate and clear.
They offered it to one who after drinking
smashed it like a jug.

Such is the father.
And he has his bread
as master in the ruddy marble-quarries.
And every woman lying-in in Pietrabianca
fears lest in the nighttime with his curses
he pass before her window, threatening.

His son, whom to the Donna Dolorosa
he dedicated in an hour of wild need,
muses in the cloistered court of the Certosa,
muses, as in a stir of reddish odors:
for his flowers all bloom red.

DER SÄNGER SINGT VOR EINEM FÜRSTENKIND

(DEM ANDENKEN VON PAULA BECKER-MODERSOHN)

Du blasses Kind, an jedem Abend soll
der Sänger dunkel stehn bei deinen Dingen
und soll dir Sagen, die im Blute klingen,
über die Brücke seiner Stimme bringen
und eine Harfe, seiner Hände voll.

Nicht aus der Zeit ist, was er dir erzählt,
gehoben ist es wie aus Wandgeweben;
solche Gestalten hat es nie gegeben;—
und Niegewesenes nennt er das Leben.
Und heute hat er diesen Sang erwählt:

Du blondes Kind von Fürsten und aus Frauen,
die einsam warteten im weissen Saal,—
fast alle waren bang, dich aufzubauen,
um aus den Bildern einst auf dich zu schauen:
auf deine Augen mit den ernsten Brauen,
auf deine Hände, hell und schmal.

Du hast von ihnen Perlen und Türkisen,
von diesen Frauen, die in Bildern stehn,
als stünden sie allein in Abendwiesen,—
du hast von ihnen Perlen und Türkisen,—
und Ringe mit verdunkelten Devisen
und Seiden, welche welke Düfte wehn.

Du trägst die Gemmen ihrer Gürtelbänder

THE SINGER SINGS BEFORE A CHILD OF PRINCES

(IN REMEMBRANCE OF PAULA BECKER-MODERSOHN)

You pale child, every evening
the singer shall stand dark among your things
and bring you legends, that ring in the blood,
over his voice's bridge
and a harp that of his hands is full.

Not out of time is that which he relates,
it is as lifted out of tapestries;
figures such as these there never were;—
and what-never-has-been he calls life.
And today he has chosen this song:

You fair-haired child of princes and out of women
who waited solitary in the white hall,—
nearly all they feared to fashion you,
some day to gaze upon you from their pictures:
upon your eyes with their earnest brows,
upon your hands, bright and slender.

You have pearls of theirs and turquoises,
from these women, standing in pictures there
as though they stood alone in evening meadows,—
you have pearls of theirs and turquoises,—
and rings with darkly dimmed devices
and silks wafting withered fragrances.

You bear the gems of their girdle-ribbons

ans hohe Fenster in den Glanz der Stunden,
und in die Seide sanfter Brautgewänder
sind deine kleinen Bücher eingebunden,
und drinnen hast du, mächtig über Länder,
ganz gross geschrieben und mit reichen, runden
Buchstaben deinen Namen vorgefunden.

Und alles ist, als wär es schon geschehn.

Sie haben so, als ob du nicht mehr kämst,
an alle Becher ihren Mund gesetzt,
zu allen Freuden ihr Gefühl gehetzt
und keinem Leide leidlos zugesehn;
so dass du jetzt
stehst und dich schämst.

. . . Du blasses Kind, dein Leben ist auch eines,—
der Sänger kommt dir sagen, dass du bist.
Und dass du mehr bist als ein Traum des Haines,
mehr als die Seligkeit des Sonnenscheines,
den mancher graue Tag vergisst.
Dein Leben ist so unaussprechlich deines,
weil es von vielen überladen ist.

Empfindest du, wie die Vergangenheiten
leicht werden, wenn du eine Weile lebst,
wie sie dich sanft auf Wunder vorbereiten,
jedes Gefühl mit Bildern dir begleiten,—

to the high window in the hours' brilliance,
and in the silk of soft bridal garments
your little books are bound,
and in them, written very large and with rich,
round letters, you, mighty over lands,
have come upon your name.

And everything is as though it had already happened.

As though you would no longer come,
to every goblet they have set their mouth,
to every joy whipped up their feeling
and at no pain looked painless on;
so that you now
stand there ashamed.

. . . You pale child, your life is also one,—
the singer comes to tell you that you are.
And that you are more than the dream of a woodland,
more than the blessedness of sunshine
which many a gray day forgets.
Your life is yours so inexpressibly
because it is with many overladen.

Are you aware how easy bygone things
become when you have lived a while,
how they prepare you quietly for wonders,
companion every feeling with a picture,—

und nur ein Zeichen scheinen ganze Zeiten
für eine Geste, die du schön erhebst.—

Das ist der Sinn von allem, was einst war,
dass es nicht bleibt mit seiner ganzen Schwere,
dass es zu unserm Wesen wiederkehre,
in uns verwoben, tief und wunderbar:
So waren diese Frauen elfenbeinern,
von vielen Rosen rötlich angeschienen,
so dunkelten die müden Königsmienen,
so wurden fahle Fürstenmunde steinern
und unbewegt von Waisen und von Weinern,
so klangen Knaben an wie Violinen
und starben für der Frauen schweres Haar;
so gingen Jungfraun der Madonna dienen,
denen die Welt verworren war.
So wurden Lauten laut und Mandolinen,
in die ein Unbekannter grösser griff,—
in warmen Samt verlief der Dolche Schliff,—
Schicksale bauten sich aus Glück und Glauben,
Abschiede schluchzten auf in Abendlauben,—
und über hundert schwarzen Eisenhauben
schwankte die Feldschlacht wie ein Schiff.
So wurden Städte langsam gross und fielen
in sich zurück wie Wellen eines Meeres,
so drängte sich zu hochbelohnten Zielen
die rasche Vogelkraft des Eisenspeeres,
so schmückten Kinder sich zu Gartenspielen,—

and but a sign whole cycles seem
for a gesture that you beautifully raise.—

This is the sense of everything that once was,
that it does not stay with its whole weight,
that it may return into our being,
woven through us, deep and wonderful:
So were these women as of ivory,
by many roses redly shone upon,
so did the weary mien of kings grow dark,
so sallow mouths of princes became stony,
unmoved by orphans and by those who wept,
so boys were resonant like violins
and died for the heavy hair of women;
so virgins went to serving the madonna,
the world confused for them.
So lutes began to sound and mandolins,
on which some unknown one more largely played,—
the gleam of daggers vanished in warm velvet,—
destinies built themselves of faith and fortune,
farewells sobbed out from evening arbors,—
and above a hundred sable iron helmets
the battle on the field swayed like a ship.
So cities slowly became great and fell
back in themselves like waves of an ocean,
so the swift bird-strength of the iron spear
hurled itself towards high-rewarded aims,
so children adorned themselves for garden games,—

und so geschah Unwichtiges und Schweres
nur, um für dieses tägliche Erleben
dir tausend grosse Gleichnisse zu geben,
an denen du gewaltig wachsen kannst.
Vergangenheiten sind dir eingepflanzt,
um sich aus dir, wie Gärten, zu erheben.

Du blasses Kind, du machst den Sänger reich
mit deinem Schicksal, das sich singen lässt:
So spiegelt sich ein grosses Gartenfest
mit vielen Lichtern im erstaunten Teich.
Im dunkeln Dichter wiederholt sich still
ein jedes Ding: ein Stern, ein Haus, ein Wald.
Und viele Dinge, die er feiern will,
umstehen deine rührende Gestalt.

so what was difficult or unimportant
happened, only to give you for this daily
living a thousand great comparisons
through which you can powerfully grow.
Past things are planted in you
that they may out of you, like gardens, rise.

You pale child, you make the singer rich
with your destiny that can so well be sung:
So a great garden festival is mirrored
with many lights in the astonished pool.
In the dark poet silently each thing
repeats itself: a star, a house, a wood.
And many things that he would celebrate
are standing round about your moving form.

THE BOOK OF PICTURES

FROM *The Second Book, Part II*

THE VOICES: NINE PAGES WITH A TITLEPAGE

TITELBLATT

Die Reichen und Glücklichen haben gut schweigen,
niemand will wissen, was sie sind.
Aber die Dürftigen müssen sich zeigen,
müssen sagen: ich bin blind,
oder: ich bin im Begriff es zu werden,
oder: es geht mir nicht gut auf Erden,
oder: ich habe ein krankes Kind,
oder: da bin ich zusammengefügt . . .

Und vielleicht, dass das gar nicht genügt.

Und weil alle sonst, wie an Dingen,
an ihnen vorbeigehn, müssen sie singen.

Und da hört man noch guten Gesang.

Freilich die Menschen sind seltsam; sie hören
lieber Kastraten in Knabenchören.

Aber Gott selber kommt und bleibt lang,
wenn ihn diese Beschnittenen stören.

TITLEPAGE

The rich and the fortunate may well keep silent,
nobody wants to know what they are.
But the needy have to reveal themselves,
have to say: I am blind,
or: I am about to become so,
or: things are not well with me on earth,
or: I have an ailing child,
or: I am patched together here . . .

And perhaps that is nowhere near enough.

And since otherwise everyone passes them by,
as they pass things, they have to sing.

And one hears some good singing then too.

Indeed people are strange; they would rather
hear castrati in boy-choirs.

But God himself comes and stays long
when these truncated ones disturb him.

DAS LIED DES BETTLERS

Ich gehe immer von Tor zu Tor,
verregnet und verbrannt;
auf einmal leg ich mein rechtes Ohr
in meine rechte Hand.
Dann kommt mir meine Stimme vor,
als hätt ich sie nie gekannt.

Dann weiss ich nicht sicher, wer da schreit,
ich oder irgendwer.
Ich schreie um eine Kleinigkeit.
Die Dichter schrein um mehr.

Und endlich mach ich noch mein Gesicht
mit beiden Augen zu;
wie's dann in der Hand liegt mit seinem Gewicht,
sieht es fast aus wie Ruh.
Damit sie nicht meinen, ich hätte nicht,
wohin ich mein Haupt tu.

THE SONG OF THE BEGGAR

I'm always going from door to door,
rained upon and scorched;
suddenly I will lay my right ear
into my right hand.
Then my voice seems to me
as though I had never known it.

Then I don't know for sure who is clamoring,
I or somebody else.
I clamor for a little mite.
The poets clamor for more.

And then I finally close my face to
with both my eyes;
as it lies in my hand then with its weight
it looks almost like rest.
So that they won't think I haven't a place
where to put my head.

DAS LIED DES BLINDEN

Ich bin blind, ihr draussen, das ist ein Fluch,
ein Widerwillen, ein Widerspruch,
etwas täglich schweres.
Ich leg meine Hand auf den Arm der Frau,
meine graue Hand auf ihr graues Grau,
und sie führt mich durch lauter Leeres.

Ihr rührt euch und rückt und bildet euch ein,
anders zu klingen als Stein auf Stein,
aber ihr irrt euch: ich allein
lebe und leide und lärme.
In mir ist ein endloses Schrein,
und ich weiss nicht, schreit mir mein
Herz oder meine Gedärme.

Erkennt ihr die Lieder? Ihr sanget sie nicht,
nicht ganz in dieser Betonung.
Euch kommt jeden Morgen das neue Licht
warm in die offene Wohnung.
Und ihr habt das Gefühl von Gesicht zu Gesicht,
und das verleitet zur Schonung.

THE SONG OF THE BLINDMAN

I am blind, you out there—that is a curse,
a contrariety, a contradiction,
something daily difficult.
I lay my hand on the arm of my wife,
my gray hand on her gray gray,
and she leads me through nothing but emptiness.

You move and shift and imagine you sound
different from stone on stone,
but you are wrong: I alone
live, am afflicted and clamor.
In me is an endless crying,
and I know not, is it my
heart cries or my bowels.

You recognize the songs? You haven't sung them,
not with this accent quite.
For you every morning the new light comes
warm in your open dwelling.
And you have the feeling of face to face,
and that tempts to forbearance.

DAS LIED DES TRINKERS

Es war nicht in mir. Es ging aus und ein.
Da wollt ich es halten. Da hielt es der Wein.
(Ich weiss nicht mehr, was es war.)
Dann hielt er mir jenes und hielt mir dies,
bis ich mich ganz auf ihn verliess.
Ich Narr.

Jetzt bin ich in seinem Spiel, und er streut
mich verächtlich herum und verliert mich noch heut
an dieses Vieh, an den Tod.
Wenn der mich, schmutzige Karte, gewinnt,
so kratzt er mit mir seinen grauen Grind
und wirft mich fort in den Kot.

THE SONG OF THE DRINKER

It was not in me. It came and went.
I wanted to hold it. It was held by wine.
(I no longer know what it was.)
Then wine held this and held that for me,
till I altogether relied on him.
Fool I.

Now I am in his game, and he scatters me
round with contempt and will lose me even today
to that brute, to death.
When he wins me, dirty card,
he will scratch his grizzly scabs with me
and throw me away in the muck.

DAS LIED DES SELBSTMÖRDERS

Also noch einen Augenblick.
Dass sie mir immer wieder den Strick
zerschneiden.
Neulich war ich so gut bereit,
und es war schon ein wenig Ewigkeit
in meinen Eingeweiden.

Halten sie mir den Löffel her,
diesen Löffel Leben.
Nein, ich will und ich will nicht mehr,
lasst mich mich übergeben.

Ich weiss, das Leben ist gar und gut,
und die Welt ist ein voller Topf,
aber mir geht es nicht ins Blut,
mir steigt es nur zu Kopf.

Andere nährt es, mich macht es krank;
begreift, das man's verschmäht.
Mindestens ein Jahrtausend lang
brauch ich jezt Diät.

THE SONG OF THE SUICIDE

Well then, another minute yet.
Again and again they manage to cut
my rope.
Recently I was so well prepared,
and there was already a little eternity
in my entrails.

They hold out the spoon to me,
that spoonful of life.
No, I don't want, I don't want any more,
only let me vomit.

I know life is well-done and good,
and the world is a full pot,
but with me it doesn't get into my blood,
it only mounts to my head.

Others it nourishes, me it makes sick;
you understand one spurns it.
For at least a thousand years now
I shall need to diet.

DAS LIED DER WITWE

Am Anfang war mir das Leben gut.
Es hielt mich warm, es machte mir Mut.
Dass es das allen Jungen tut,
wie konnt ich das damals wissen.
Ich wusste nicht was das Leben war—,
auf einmal war es nur Jahr um Jahr,
nicht mehr gut, nicht mehr neu, nicht mehr wunderbar,
wie mitten entzweigerissen.

Das war nicht seine, nicht meine Schuld;
wir hatten beide nichts als Geduld,
aber der Tod hat keine.
Ich sah ihn kommen (wie schlecht er kam),
und ich schaute ihm zu, wie er nahm und nahm:
es war ja gar nicht das Meine.

Was war denn das Meine; Meines, mein?
War mir nicht selbst mein Elendsein
nur vom Schicksal geliehn?
Das Schicksal will nicht nur das Glück,
es will die Pein und das Schrein zurück,
und es kauft für alt den Ruin.

Das Schicksal war da und erwarb für ein Nichts
jeden Ausdruck meines Gesichts,
bis auf die Art zu gehn.
Das war ein täglicher Ausverkauf,
und als ich leer war, gab es mich auf
und liess mich offen stehn.

THE SONG OF THE WIDOW

Life was good to me in the beginning.
It kept me warm, it gave me zest.
That it does so to all the young,
how could I know that then?
I did not know what living was—,
suddenly it was just year on year,
no more good, no more new, no more wonderful,
as if torn in two in the middle.

That was not his fault and not mine;
we both had nothing but patience;
but death has none.
I saw him coming (how mean he came),
and I watched him as he took and took:
it wasn't mine at all.

What then was mine; my own, mine?
Was not even my being wretched
only loaned me by fate?
Fate wants not only the happiness,
it wants the pain back and the crying,
and it buys the ruin for old.

Fate was there and acquired for a nothing
every expression of my face,
even to my way of walking.
That was a daily selling out,
and when I was empty it gave me up
and left me standing open.

DAS LIED DES IDIOTEN

Sie hindern mich nicht. Sie lassen mich gehn.
Sie sagen, es könne nichts geschehn.
Wie gut.
Es kann nichts geschehn. Alles kommt und kreist
immerfort um den Heiligen Geist,
um den gewissen Geist (du weisst)—,
wie gut.

Nein, man muss wirklich nicht meinen, es sei
irgendeine Gefahr dabei.
Da ist freilich das Blut.
Das Blut ist das Schwerste. Das Blut ist schwer,
manchmal glaub ich, ich kann nicht mehr—.
(Wie gut.)

Ah, was ist das für ein schöner Ball;
rot und rund wie ein Überall.
Gut, dass ihr ihn erschuft.
Ob der wohl kommt, wenn man ruft?

Wie sich das alles seltsam benimmt,
ineinandertreibt, auseinanderschwimmt:
freundlich, ein wenig unbestimmt;
wie gut.

THE SONG OF THE IDIOT

They do not hinder me. They let me go.
They say that nothing can happen.
How good.
Nothing can happen. All things come and circle
constantly round the Holy Ghost,
round the certain spirit (you know)—,
how good.

No, one must really not think that there is
danger in it of any sort.
Of course there's the blood.
The blood is the heaviest. The blood is heavy,
sometimes I think I cannot go on—.
(How good.)

Ah, what a beautiful ball that is;
red and round as an everywhere.
Good, that you created it.
Wonder if it comes when one calls?

How oddly all that behaves,
running together, swimming apart:
friendly, a little indefinite;
how good.

DAS LIED DER WAISE

Ich bin niemand und werde auch niemand sein.
Jetzt bin ich ja zum Sein noch zu klein;
aber auch später.

Mütter und Väter,
erbarmt euch mein.

Zwar es lohnt nicht des Pflegens Müh:
ich werde doch gemäht.
Mich kann keiner brauchen: jetzt ist es zu früh,
und morgen ist es zu spät.

Ich habe nur dieses eine Kleid,
es wird dünn, und es verbleicht,
aber es hält eine Ewigkeit
auch noch vor Gott vielleicht.

Ich habe nur dieses bisschen Haar
(immer dasselbe blieb),
das einmal Eines Liebstes war.

Nun hat er nichts mehr lieb.

THE SONG OF THE ORPHAN

I am nobody and neither shall I be anybody.
Now of course I am still too small for being;
but later too.

Mothers and fathers,
have pity on me.

Indeed it's not worth the trouble of rearing **me:**
I shall be mowed down all the same.
No one can use me: it's too early now,
and tomorrow it will be too late.

I have only this one dress,
it's wearing thin, and it's fading,
but it will last an eternity
even before God perhaps.

I have only this bit of hair
(the same always remained),
that once was somebody's dearest.

Now he loves nothing any more.

DAS LIED DES ZWERGES

Meine Seele ist vielleicht grad und gut;
aber mein Herz, mein verbogenes Blut,
alles das was mir wehe tut,
kann sie nicht aufrecht tragen.
Sie hat keinen Garten, sie hat kein Bett,
sie hängt an meinem scharfen Skelett
mit entsetztem Flügelschlagen.

Aus meinen Händen wird auch nichts mehr.
Wie verkümmert sie sind, sieh her:
zähe hüpfen sie, feucht und schwer,
wie kleine Kröten nach Regen.
Und das andere an mir ist
abgetragen und alt und trist;
warum zögert Gott, auf den Mist
alles das hinzulegen.

Ob er mir zürnt für mein Gesicht
mit dem mürrischen Munde?
Es war ja so oft bereit, ganz licht
und klar zu werden im Grunde;
aber nichts kam ihm je so dicht
wie die grossen Hunde.
Und die Hunde haben das nicht.

THE SONG OF THE DWARF

My soul is perhaps straight and good;
but my heart, my distorted blood,
everything that is hurting me,
it cannot carry upright.
It has no garden, it has no bed,
it hangs on my sharp skeleton
with terrified beating of wings.

Nor will anything come of my hands any more.
How stunted they are, see here:
clammy they hop, heavy and moist,
like little toads after rain.
And the other things about me are
threadbare and old and triste;
why does God hesitate to lay
it all on the dungheap?

Is he angry with me for my face
with its mumpish mouth?
So often it was ready to turn
all light and clear in its depths:
but nothing ever came so close
to it as big dogs did.
And dogs do not have that.

DAS LIED DES AUSSÄTZIGEN

Sieh, ich bin einer, den alles verlassen hat.
Keiner weiss in der Stadt von mir,
Aussatz hat mich befallen.
Und ich schlage mein Klapperwerk,
klopfe mein trauriges Augenmerk
in die Ohren allen,
die nahe vorübergehn.
Und die es hölzern hören, sehn
erst gar nicht her, und was hier geschehn,
wollen sie nicht erfahren.

Soweit der Klang meiner Klapper reicht,
bin ich zu Hause; aber vielleicht
machst du meine Klapper so laut,
dass sich keiner in meine Ferne traut,
der mir jetzt aus der Nähe weicht.
So dass ich sehr lange gehen kann,
ohne Mädchen, Frau oder Mann
oder Kind zu entdecken.

Tiere will ich nicht schrecken.

THE SONG OF THE LEPER

See, I am one whom all have deserted.
No one knows of me in the city,
leprosy has befallen me.
And I beat upon my rattle,
knock the sorrowful sight of me
into the ears of all
who pass near by.
And those who woodenly hear it, look
not this way at all, and what's happened here
they do not want to learn.

As far as the sound of my clapper reaches
I am at home; but perhaps
you are making my clapper so loud
that none will trust himself far from me
who now shuns coming near.
So that I can go a very long way
without discovering girl or woman
or man or child.

I would not frighten animals.

REQUIEM

(Dedicated to Clara Westhoff)

Seit einer Stunde ist um ein Ding menr
auf Erden. Mehr um einen Kranz.
Vor einer Weile war das leichtes Laub . . . Ich wands:
und jetzt ist dieser Efeu seltsam schwer
und so von Dunkel voll, als tränke er
aus meinen Dingen zukünftige Nächte.
Jetzt graut mir fast vor dieser nächsten Nacht,
allein mit diesem Kranz, den ich gemacht,
nicht ahnend, dass da etwas wird,
wenn sich die Ranken ründen um den Reifen;
ganz nur bedürftig, dieses zu begreifen:
dass etwas nicht mehr sein kann. Wie verirrt
in nie betretene Gedanken, darinnen wunderliche Dinge stehn,
die ich schon einmal gesehen haben muss . . .

. . . Flussabwärts treiben die Blumen, welche die Kinder
gerissen haben im Spiel; aus den offenen Fingern fiel
eine und eine, bis der Strauss nicht mehr zu erkennen war.
Bis der Rest, den sie nach Haus gebracht, gerade gut zum
verbrennen war. Dann konnte man ja die ganze Nacht, wenn
einen alle schlafen meinen, um die gebrochenen Blumen
weinen.

Gretel, von allem Anbeginn
war dir bestimmt, sehr zeitig zu sterben,
blond zu sterben.
Lange schon, eh dir zu leben bestimmt war.
Darum stellte der Herr eine Schwester vor dich
und dann einen Bruder,
damit vor dir wären zwei Nahe, zwei Reine,

Since the last hour there is more on earth
by one thing. More by a wreath.
A while ago it was light foliage . . . I wound it:
and now this ivy is singularly heavy
and as full of dark as though it drank
out of my things future nights.
I almost shudder now at this next night,
alone with this wreath that I made
not guessing that something comes about
when the tendrils ring themselves around the hoop;
wholly needing to understand but this:
that something can be no more. As though astray
in never entered thoughts, in which stand wondrous things
I must already once have seen . . .

. . . Downstream drift the flowers that the children
have snatched in their play; from their open fingers
one fell and one, till the nosegay was no more to be
recognized. Till the remnant they brought home was
just fit for burning. Then of course the whole night, when
all think one asleep, one could weep for the broken
flowers.

Gretel, from earliest beginning
it was decreed you should die betimes,
die fair.
Long already, ere it was decreed you should live.
Therefore the Lord set a sister before you
and then a brother,
that before you might be two near, two pure ones,

welche das Sterben dir zeigten,
das deine:
dein Sterben.
Deine Geschwister wurden erfunden,
nur, damit du dich dran gewöhntest
und dich an zweien Sterbestunden
mit der dritten versöhntest,
die dir seit Jahrtausenden droht.
Für deinen Tod
sind Leben erstanden;
Hände, welche Blüten banden,
Blicke, welche die Rosen rot
und die Menschen mächtig empfanden,
hat man gebildet und wieder vernichtet
und hat zweimal das Sterben gedichtet,
eh es, gegen dich selbst gerichtet,
aus der verloschenen Bühne trat.

. . . Nahte es dir schrecklich, geliebte Gespielin?
war es dein Feind?
Hast du dich ihm ans Herz geweint?
Hat es dich aus den heissen Kissen
in die flackernde Nacht gerissen,
in der niemand schlief im ganzen Haus . . . ?
Wie sah es aus?
Du musst es wissen . . .
Du bist dazu in die Heimat gereist.

. . . .

Du weisst,
wie die Mandeln blühn,

who should show you death,
yours:
your dying.
Your sister and brother were invented
only that you might get used to it
and to the death-hours of two
reconcile yourself with the third,
which for millenniums has threatened you.
For your death
lives came into being;
hands that bound blossoms,
glances that found roses red
and mankind mighty
were formed and annulled again,
and twice was the drama of dying written
ere, against yourself directed,
it stepped from the extinguished stage.

. . . Did it near you terribly, playmate beloved?
was it your enemy?
Did you weep yourself to its heart?
Did it tear you out of the hot pillows
into the flickering night
in which no one slept in the whole house . . . ?
How did it look?
You must know . . .
For that you had traveled home.

. . . .

You know
how the almonds bloom,

und dass Seeen blau sind.
Viele Dinge, die nur im Gefühle der Frau sind,
welche die erste Liebe erfuhr,
weisst du. Dir flüsterte die Natur
in des Südens spätdämmernden Tagen
so unendliche Schönheit ein,
wie sonst nur selige Lippen sie sagen
seliger Menschen, die zu zwein
eine Welt haben und eine Stimme—
leiser hast du das alles gespürt,—
(o wie hat das unendlich Grimme
deine unendliche Demut berührt).
Deine Briefe kamen von Süden,
warm noch von Sonne, aber verwaist,—
endlich bist du selbst deinen müden
bittenden Briefen nachgereist;
denn du warst nicht gerne im Glanze,
jede Farbe lag auf dir wie Schuld,
und du lebtest in Ungeduld,
denn du wusstest: Das ist nicht das Ganze.
Leben ist nur ein Teil . . . Wovon?
Leben ist nur ein Ton . . . Worin?
Leben hat Sinn nur verbunden mit vielen
Kreisen des weithin wachsenden Raumes,—
Leben ist so nur der Traum eines Traumes,
aber Wachsein ist anderswo.
So liessest du's los.
Gross liessest du's los.
Und wir kannten dich klein.
Dein war so wenig: ein Lächeln, ein kleines,

and that lakes are blue.
Many things felt only by the woman
who has known first love,
you know. Nature whispered to you
in the South's late-fading days
beauty so endless
as else only the happy lips
of happy people say, who, two by two,
have one world and one voice—
more gently you sensed all that,—
(o how the unendingly grim
touched your unending humility).
Your letters came from the South,
warm still with sun, but orphaned,—
at last you yourself followed after
your weary beseeching letters;
for you did not like being in the light,
every color lay on you like guilt,
and you lived in impatience,
for you knew: This is not the whole.
Living is only a part . . . what of?
Living is only a tone . . . what in?
Living has sense only joined with many
circles of far-increasing space,—
Living is thus but the dream of a dream,
but awakeness is elsewhere.
So you let it go.
Greatly you let it go.
And we knew you as small.
So little was yours: a smile, a little one,

ein bischen melancholisch schon immer,
sehr sanftes Haar und ein kleines Zimmer
das dir seit dem Tode der Schwester weit war.
Als ob alles andere nur dein Kleid war,
so scheint es mir jetzt, du stilles Gespiel.
Aber sehr viel
warst du. Und wir wusstens manchmal,
wenn du am Abend kamst in den Saal;
wussten manchmal: jetzt müsste man beten;
eine Menge ist eingetreten,
eine Menge, welche dir nachgeht,
weil du den Weg weisst.
Und du hast ihn wissen gemusst
und hast ihn gewusst
gestern . . .
Jüngste der Schwestern.

Sieh her,
dieser Kranz ist so schwer.
Und sie werden ihn auf dich legen,
diesen schweren Kranz.
Kanns dein Sarg aushalten?
Wenn er bricht
unter dem schwarzen Gewicht,
kriecht in die Falten
von deinem Kleid
Efeu.
Weit rankt er hinauf,
rings rankt er dich um,
und der Saft, der sich in seinen Ranken bewegt,

always a trifle melancholy already,
very soft hair and a small room
that was wide for you since your sister's death.
As though everything else were but your dress,
so it seems to me now, you quiet playmate.
But very much
You were. And we knew it sometimes,
when at evening you came into the room;
knew sometimes: now one should pray;
a multitude has entered,
a multitude that follows you
because you know the way.
And you had to know it
and did know it
yesterday . . .
youngest of the sisters.

See here,
this wreath is so heavy.
And they will lay it upon you,
this heavy wreath.
Can your coffin endure it?
If it breaks
under the black weight,
into the folds of your dress
will creep
ivy.
Far up will it twine,
all around you will it twine,
and the sap that stirs in its tendrils

regt dich auf mit seinem Geräusch;
so keusch bist du.
Aber du bist nicht mehr zu.
Langgedehnt bist du und lass.
Deines Leibes Türen sind angelehnt,
und nass
tritt der Efeu ein . . .

· · · · · · · · · ·

Wie Reihn
von Nonnen,
die sich führen
an schwarzem Seil,
weil es dunkel ist in dir, du Bronnen.
In den leeren Gängen
deines Blutes drängen sie zu deinem Herzen;
wo sonst deine sanften Schmerzen
sich begegneten mit bleichen
Freuden und Erinnerungen,
wandeln sie wie im Gebet
in das Herz, das, ganz verklungen,
dunkel, allen offen steht.
Aber dieser Kranz ist schwer
nur im Licht,
nur unter Lebenden, hier bei mir;
und sein Gewicht
ist nicht mehr,
wenn ich ihn zu dir legen werde.
Die Erde ist voller Gleichgewicht,
deine Erde.
Er ist schwer von meinen Augen, die daran hängen,

will excite you with its rustle;
so chaste are you.
But you are closed no more.
Long-stretched you lie and slack.
Your body's doors lean on the latch,
and wet
the ivy enters . . .

. . . .

Like rows
of nuns,
who guide themselves
by a black rope,
for it is dark in you, you well.
In the empty corridors
of your blood they press towards your heart;
where else your gentle sorrows
met with pale
joys and memories,
they wander as in prayer
in the heart that, wholly stilled,
dark, to all stands open.
But this wreath is heavy
only in the light,
only among living ones, here with me;
and its weight
will be no more
when I shall lay it down by you.
The earth is full of equipoise,
your earth.
This wreath is heavy with my eyes that hang upon it,

schwer von den Gängen,
die ich um ihn getan;
Ängste aller, welche ihn sahn,
haften daran.
Nimm ihn zu dir, denn er ist dein,
seit er ganz fertig ist.
Nimm ihn von mir.
Lass mich allein! Er ist wie ein Gast . . .
Fast schäm ich mich seiner.
Hast du auch Furcht, Gretel?

Du kannst nicht mehr gehn?
Kannst nicht mehr bei mir in der Stube stehn?
Tun dir die Füsse weh?
So bleib, wo jetzt alle beisammen sind,
man wird ihn dir morgen bringen, mein Kind,
durch die entlaubte Allee.
Man wird ihn dir bringen, warte getrost,—
man bringt dir morgen noch mehr.

Wenn es auch morgen tobt und tost,
das schadet den Blumen nicht sehr.
Man wird sie dir bringen. Du hast das Recht,
sie sicher zu haben, mein Kind,
und wenn sie auch morgen schwarz und schlecht
und lange vergangen sind.
Sei deshalb nicht bange. Du wirst nicht mehr
unterscheiden, was steigt oder sinkt;
die Farben sind zu, und die Töne sind leer,
und du wirst auch gar nicht mehr wissen, wer

heavy with the walking
I have done for it.
Fears of all who saw it
cling to it.
Take it to you, for it is yours
since it is all finished.
Take it from me.
Leave me alone! It is like a guest . . .
I am almost ashamed of it.
Are you afraid too, Gretel?

You can walk no more?
Stand here no more in my room?
Do your feet hurt?
Then stay, where all are together now,
they will bring it to you tomorrow, my child,
through the leaf-stripped avenue.
They will bring it to you, wait with good cheer,—
tomorrow they will bring you yet more.

Even if it storm and rage tomorrow,
that will not hurt the flowers much.
They will be brought to you. You have the right
surely to have them, my child,
and even if tomorrow they are black and bad
and faded long ago.
Fear not for that. You will no longer
distinguish what rises or falls;
colors are closed, and tones are empty,
nor will you know any more at all

dir alle die Blumen bringt.

Jetzt weisst du das andre, das uns verstösst,
sooft wirs im Dunkel erfasst;
von dem, was du sehntest, bist du erlöst
zu etwas, was du hast.
Unter uns warst du von kleiner Gestalt,
vielleicht bist du jetzt ein erwachsener Wald
mit Winden und Stimmen im Laub.—
Glaub mir, Gespiel, dir geschah nicht Gewalt:
dein Tod war schon alt,
als dein Leben begann;
drum griff er es an,
damit es ihn nicht überlebte.

Schwebte etwas um mich?
Trat Nachtwind herein?
Ich bebte nicht.
Ich bin stark und allein.—
Was hab ich heute geschafft?
. . . Efeulaub holt ich am Abend und wands
und bog es zusammen, bis es ganz gehorchte.
Noch glänzt es mit schwarzem Glanz.
Und meine Kraft
kreist in dem Kranz.

who brings you all the flowers.

Now you know that other which rebuffs us
whenever we've grasped it in the dark;
from what you longed for you are released
to something that you have.
Among us you were small of stature;
perhaps you are now a full-grown wood
with winds and voices in its leaves.—
Believe me, playmate, no violence was done you:
your death was already old
when your life began;
therefore he seized it,
that it should not outlive him.

Did something hover round me?
Did nightwind enter?
I did not quake.
I am strong and alone.—
What have I done today?
. . . Ivy I fetched at evening and wound it
and bent it together, till it wholly obeyed me.
It still gleams with a black gleam.
And my strength
circles in the wreath.

SCHLUSSSTÜCK

Der Tod ist gross.
Wir sind die Seinen
lachenden Munds.
Wenn wir uns mitten im Leben meinen,
wagt er zu weinen
mitten in uns.

CLOSING PIECE

Death is great.
We are his
with laughing mouth.
When we think ourselves in the midst of life,
he dares to weep
in the midst of us.

✎》《✎

NEW POEMS

FROM *Part I*

✎》《✎

FRÜHER APOLLO

Wie manchesmal durch das noch unbelaubte
Gezweig ein Morgen durchsieht, der schon ganz
im Frühling ist: so ist in seinem Haupte
nichts, was verhindern könnte, das der Glanz

aller Gedichte uns fast tödlich träfe;
denn noch kein Schatten ist in seinem Schaun,
zu kühl für Lorbeer sind noch seine Schläfe,
und später erst wird aus den Augenbrau'n

hochstämmig sich der Rosengarten heben,
aus welchem Blätter, einzeln, ausgelöst
hintreiben werden auf des Mundes Beben,

der jetzt noch still ist, niegebraucht und blinkend
und nur mit seinem Lächeln etwas trinkend,
als würde ihm sein Singen eingeflösst.

EARLY APOLLO

As many a time through the yet unleaved
branches a morn looks through that is already
all in spring: so is there in his head
naught that could hinder the glory of all poems

from falling almost fatally upon us;
for yet no shadow is there in his gaze,
too cool for laurel are his temples still,
and only later from his eyebrows shall

tall-stemmed the rose-garden lift itself,
out of which petals, separately, released
will drift upon the quivering of his mouth,

that yet is quiet, never-used and gleaming
and only drinking something with its smile,
as though its singing were being infused in it.

LIEBESLIED

Wie soll ich meine Seele halten, dass
sie nicht an deine rührt? Wie soll ich sie
hinheben über dich zu andern Dingen?
Ach gerne möcht ich sie bei irgendetwas
Verlorenem im Dunkel unterbringen
an einer fremden stillen Stelle, die
nicht weiterschwingt, wenn deine Tiefen schwingen.
Doch alles, was uns anrührt, dich und mich,
nimmt uns zusammen wie ein Bogenstrich,
der aus zwei Saiten eine Stimme zieht.
Auf welches Instrument sind wir gespannt?
Und welcher Spieler hat uns in der Hand?
O süsses Lied.

LOVESONG

How shall I withhold my soul so that
it does not touch on yours? How shall I
uplift it over you to other things?
Ah willingly would I by some
lost thing in the dark give it harbor
in an unfamiliar silent place
that does not vibrate on when your depths vibrate.
Yet everything that touches us, you and me,
takes us together as a bow's stroke does,
that out of two strings draws a single voice.
Upon what instrument are we two spanned?
And what player has us in his hand?
O sweet song.

DER ÖLBAUMGARTEN

Er ging hinauf unter dem grauen Laub
ganz grau und aufgelöst im Ölgelände
und legte seine Stirne voller Staub
tief in das Staubigsein der heissen Hände.

Nach allem dies. Und dieses war der Schluss.
Jetzt soll ich gehen, während ich erblinde,
und warum willst Du, dass ich sagen muss,
Du seist, wenn ich dich selber nicht mehr finde.

Ich finde Dich nicht mehr. Nicht in mir, nein.
Nicht in den andern. Nicht in diesem Stein.
Ich finde Dich nicht mehr. Ich bin allein.

Ich bin allein mit aller Menschen Gram,
den ich durch Dich zu lindern unternahm,
der Du nicht bist. O namenlose Scham . . .

Später erzählte man: ein Engel kam—.

Warum ein Engel? Ach es kam die Nacht
und blätterte gleichgültig in den Bäumen.
Die Jünger rührten sich in ihren Träumen.
Warum ein Engel? Ach es kam die Nacht.

Die Nacht. die kam, war keine ungemeine;

THE GARDEN OF OLIVES

He went up under the gray foliage
all gray and merging with the olive lands
and laid his forehead that was full of dust
deep in the dustiness of his hot hands.

After everything this. And this was the end.
Now I must go, while I am turning blind,
and why dost Thou so will, that I must say
Thou art, when I myself do no more find Thee.

I find Thee no more. Not within me, no.
Not in the others. Not within this rock.
I find Thee no more. I am alone.

I am alone with all mankind's grief,
which I through Thee to lighten undertook,
Thou who art not. O nameless shame . . .

Later it was said: an angel came—.

Why an angel? Alas it was the night
leafing indifferently among the trees.
The disciples stirred in their dreams.
Why an angel? Alas it was the night.

The night that came was no uncommon night;

so gehen hunderte vorbei.
Da schlafen Hunde, und da liegen Steine.
Ach eine traurige, ach irgendeine,
die wartet, bis es wieder Morgen sei.

Denn Engel kommen nicht zu solchen Betern,
und Nächte werden nicht um solche gross.
Die Sich-Verlierenden lässt alles los,
und sie sind preisgegeben von den Vätern
und ausgeschlossen aus der Mütter Schoss.

hundreds like it go by.
Then dogs sleep, and then stones lie.
Alas a sad night, alas any night
that waits till it be morning once again.

For angels come not to such suppliants,
and nights do not round about such grow large.
Who lose themselves by all things are let go,
and they are abandoned of their fathers
and shut out of their mothers' womb.

DER PANTHER

IM JARDIN DES PLANTES, PARIS

Sein Blick ist vom Vorübergehn der Stäbe
so müd geworden, dass es nichts mehr hält.
Ihm ist, als ob es tausend Stäbe gäbe
und hinter tausend Stäben keine Welt.

Der weiche Gang geschmeidig starker Schritte,
der sich im allerkleinsten Kreise dreht,
ist wie ein Tanz von Kraft um eine Mitte,
in der betäubt ein grosser Wille steht.

Nur manchmal schiebt der Vorhang der Pupille
sich lautlos auf—. Dann geht ein Bild hinein,
geht durch der Glieder angespannte Stille—
und hört im Herzen auf zu sein.

THE PANTHER

JARDIN DES PLANTES, PARIS

His vision from the passing of the bars
is grown so weary that it holds no more.
To him it seems there are a thousand bars
and behind a thousand bars no world.

The padding gait of flexibly strong strides,
that in the very smallest circle turns,
is like a dance of strength around a center
in which stupefied a great will stands.

Only sometimes the curtain of the pupil
soundlessly parts—. Then an image enters,
goes through the tensioned stillness of the limbs—
and in the heart ceases to be.

SANKT SEBASTIAN

Wie ein Liegender so steht er; ganz
hingehalten von dem grossen Willen.
Weit entrückt wie Mütter, wenn sie stillen,
und in sich gebunden wie ein Kranz.

Und die Pfeile kommen: jetzt und jetzt
und als sprängen sie aus seinen Lenden,
eisen bebend mit den freien Enden.
Doch er lächelt dunkel, unverletzt.

Einmal nur wird eine Trauer gross,
und die Augen liegen schmerzlich bloss,
bis sie etwas leugnen, wie Geringes,
und als liessen sie verächtlich los
die Vernichter eines schönen Dinges.

SAINT SEBASTIAN

Like one recumbent, so he stands; all
sustained by his great will.
Far withdrawn like mothers, when they suckle,
and bound into himself like a wreath.

And the arrows come: now and now
and as if they sprang out of his loins,
ironly quivering with their free ends.
Yet he is smiling darkly, and uninjured.

Only once a sorrowing grows big,
and his eyes lie painfully bared, until
they disavow something, as it were petty,
and as though they scornfully let go
the destroyers of a lovely thing.

DER SCHWAN

Diese Mühsal, durch noch Ungetanes
schwer und wie gebunden hinzugehn,
gleicht dem ungeschaffnen Gang des Schwanes.

Und das Sterben, dieses Nichtmehrfassen
jenes Grunds, auf dem wir täglich stehn,
seinem ängstlichen Sich-Niederlassen—:

in die Wasser, die ihn sanft empfangen
und die sich, wie glücklich und vergangen,
unter ihm zurückziehn, Flut um Flut;
während er unendlich still und sicher
immer mündiger und königlicher
und gelassener zu ziehn geruht.

THE SWAN

This toiling to go through something yet
undone, heavily and as though in bonds,
is like the ungainly gait of the swan.

And dying, this no longer grasping
of that ground on which we daily stand,
like his anxious letting-himself-down—:

into the waters, which receive him smoothly
and which, as though happy and bygone,
draw back underneath him, flow on flow;
while he, infinitely still and sure,
ever more maturely and more royally
and more serenely deigns to draw along.

DIE ERBLINDENDE

Sie sass so wie die anderen beim Tee.
Mir war zuerst, als ob sie ihre Tasse
ein wenig anders als die andern fasse.
Sie lächelte einmal. Es tat fast weh.

Und als man schliesslich sich erhob und sprach
und langsam und wie es der Zufall brachte
durch viele Zimmer ging (man sprach und lachte),
da sah ich sie. Sie ging den andern nach,

verhalten, so wie eine, welche gleich
wird singen müssen und vor vielen Leuten;
auf ihren hellen Augen, die sich freuten,
war Licht von aussen wie auf einem Teich.

Sie folgte langsam, und sie brauchte lang,
als wäre etwas noch nicht überstiegen;
und doch: als ob, nach einem Ubergang,
sie nicht mehr gehen würde, sondern fliegen.

GOING BLIND

She sat quite like the others there at tea.
It seemed to me at first she grasped her cup
a little differently from the rest.
Once she gave a smile. It almost hurt.

And when people finally stood up and spoke
and slowly and as chance brought it about
moved through many rooms (they talked and laughed),
I saw her. She was moving after the others,

withheld, as one who in a moment
will have to sing and before many people;
upon her bright eyes, that rejoiced,
was light from outside as upon a pool.

She followed slowly, taking a long time,
as though something had not yet been surmounted;
and yet as though, after a crossing over,
she would no longer walk, but fly.

LETZTER ABEND

Und Nacht und fernes Fahren; denn der Train
des ganzen Heeres zog am Park vorüber.
Er aber hob den Blick vom Clavecin
und spielte noch und sah zu ihr hinüber

beinah, wie man in einen Spiegel schaut:
so sehr erfüllt von seinen jungen Zügen
und wissend, wie sie seine Trauer trügen,
schön und verführender bei jedem Laut.

Doch plötzlich wars, als ob das sich verwische:
sie stand wie mühsam in der Fensternische
und hielt des Herzens drängendes Geklopf.

Sein Spiel gab nach. Von draussen wehte Frische.
Und seltsam fremd stand auf dem Spiegeltische
der schwarze Tschako mit dem Totenkopf.

THE LAST EVENING

And night and distant faring; for the transport
of the whole army was moving by the park.
But he raised his eyes from the clavecin
and went on playing and looked across at her

almost as one gazes in a mirror:
so deeply filled with his young features
and knowing how they would bear his sorrow,
beautiful and more seductive with each sound.

Yet suddenly it seemed as if that was blurring:
she stood as with effort in the window-niche
and held the urgent beating of her heart.

His playing gave way. From outside freshness drifted.
And curiously alien on the console
stood the black shako with the death's-head.

JUGENDBILDNIS MEINES VATERS

Im Auge Traum. Die Stirn wie in Berührung
mit etwas Fernem. Um den Mund enorm
viel Jugend, ungelächelte Verführung,
und vor der vollen schmückenden Verschnürung
der schlanken adeligen Uniform
der Säbelkorb und beide Hände—, die
abwarten, ruhig, zu nichts hingedrängt.
Und nun fast nicht mehr sichtbar: als ob sie
zuerst, die Fernes greifenden, verschwänden.
Und alles andre mit sich selbst verhängt
und ausgelöscht, als ob wir's nicht verständen,
und tief aus seiner eignen Tiefe trüb—.

Du schnell vergehendes Daguerreotyp
in meinen langsamer vergehenden Händen.

YOUTHFUL PORTRAIT OF MY FATHER

In the eyes dream. The forehead as in touch
with something far. About the mouth enormously
much youth, unsmiled seductiveness,
and before the full ornamental lacings
of the slim aristocratic uniform
the saber's basket-hilt and both the hands—,
that wait, quietly, impelled towards nothing.
And now scarce longer visible: as though they
first, seizers of far things, would disappear.
And all the rest curtained with itself
and effaced, as though we could not understand it,
and clouded deep out of its own depths—.

You swiftly fading daguerreotype
in my more slowly fading hands.

SELBSTBILDNIS AUS DEM JAHRE 1906

Des alten lange adligen Geschlechtes
Feststehendes im Augenbogenbau.
Im Blicke noch der Kindheit Angst und Blau
und Demut da und dort, nicht eines Knechtes,
doch eines Dienenden und einer Frau.
Der Mund als Mund gemacht, gross und genau,
nicht überredend, aber ein Gerechtes
Aussagendes. Die Stirne ohne Schlechtes
und gern im Schatten stiller Niederschau.

Das, als Zusammenhang, erst nur geahnt;
noch nie im Leiden oder im Gelingen
zusammgefasst zu dauerndem Durchdringen,
doch so, als wäre mit zerstreuten Dingen
von fern ein Ernstes, Wirkliches geplant.

SELF-PORTRAIT FROM THE YEAR 1906

The old long-noble generation's
steadfastness in the eyebrow's build.
In the glance still childhood's fear and blue
and humility here and there, not of a servile sort,
yet of one who serves and of a woman.
The mouth made as a mouth, large and defined,
not persuasive, but in a just behalf
affirmative. The forehead without guile,
liking the shade of quiet downward-gazing.

This, as assembled whole, only just sensed;
never yet in sorrow or success
gathered to enduring attainment,
yet such as though from afar with scattered things
something serious, real were being planned.

DAS KARUSSELL

JARDIN DU LUXEMBOURG

Mit einem Dach und seinem Schatten dreht
sich eine kleine Weile der Bestand
von bunten Pferden, alle aus dem Land,
das lange zögert, eh es untergeht.
Zwar manche sind an Wagen angespannt,
doch alle haben Mut in ihren Mienen;
ein böser roter Löwe geht mit ihnen
und dann und wann ein weisser Elefant.

Sogar ein Hirsch ist da ganz wie im Wald,
nur dass er einen Sattel trägt und drüber
ein kleines blaues Mädchen aufgeschnallt.

Und auf dem Löwen reitet weiss ein Junge
und hält sich mit der kleinen heissen Hand,
dieweil der Löwe Zähne zeigt und Zunge.

Und dann und wann ein weisser Elefant.

Und auf den Pferden kommen sie vorüber,
auch Mädchen, helle, diesem Pferdesprunge
fast schon entwachsen; mitten in dem Schwunge
schauen sie auf, irgendwohin, herüber—

Und dann und wann ein weisser Elefant.

Und das geht hin und eilt sich, dass es endet,

THE CAROUSEL

JARDIN DU LUXEMBOURG

With a roof and its shadow it rotates
a little while, the herd of particolored
horses, all from the land
that lingers long ere it sinks out of sight.
Some it is true are hitched to carriages,
yet all of them have mettle in their mien;
a vicious red lion goes with them
and every now and then a white elephant.

Even a deer is there quite as in the woods,
save that he bears a saddle and on that
a little blue girl buckled up.

And on the lion rides all white a boy
and holds himself with his small hot hand,
the while the lion shows his teeth and tongue.

And every now and then a white elephant.

And on the horses they come passing by,
girls too, bright girls, who almost have outgrown
this leap of horses; midway in their swing
they look up, anywhere, across—

And every now and then a white elephant.

And this goes on and hurries that it may end,

und kreist und dreht sich nur und hat kein Ziel.
Ein Rot, ein Grün, ein Grau vorbeigesendet,
ein kleines kaum begonnenes Profil.
Und manchesmal ein Lächeln, hergewendet,
ein seliges, das blendet und verschwendet
an dieses atemlose blinde Spiel.

and only circles and turns and has no goal.
A red, a green, a gray being sent by,
some little profile hardly yet begun.
And occasionally a smile, turning this way,
a happy one, that dazzles and dissipates
over this blind and breathless game.

SPANISCHE TÄNZERIN

Wie in der Hand ein Schwefelzündholz, weiss,
eh es zur Flamme kommt, nach allen Seiten
zuckende Zungen streckt—: beginnt im Kreis
naher Beschauer hastig, hell und heiss
ihr runder Tanz sich zuckend auszubreiten.

Und plötzlich ist er Flamme ganz und gar.

Mit ihrem Blick entzündet sie ihr Haar
und dreht auf einmal mit gewagter Kunst
ihr ganzes Kleid in diese Feuersbrunst,
aus welcher sich, wie Schlangen, die erschrecken,
die nackte Arme wach und klappernd strecken.

Und dann: als wurde ihr das Feuer knapp,
nimmt sie es ganz zusamm und wirft es ab
sehr herrisch, mit hochmütiger Gebärde
und schaut: da liegt es rasend auf der Erde
und flammt noch immer und ergibt sich nicht—.
Doch sieghaft, sicher und mit einem süssen
grüssenden Lächeln hebt sie ihr Gesicht
und stampft es aus mit kleinen festen Füssen.

SPANISH DANCER

As in one's hand a sulphur match, whitely,
before it comes aflame, to every side
darts twitching tongues—: within the circle
of close watchers hasty, bright and hot
her round dance begins twitching to spread itself.

And suddenly it is altogether flame.

With her glance she sets alight her hair
and all at once with daring art
whirls her whole dress within this conflagration,
out of which her naked arms upstretch
like startled snakes awake and rattling.

And then: as though the fire were tightening round her,
she gathers it all in one and casts it off
very haughtily, with imperious gesture
and watches: it lies there raging on the ground
and still flames and will not give in—.
Yet conquering, sure and with a sweet
greeting smile she lifts her countenance
and stamps it out with little sturdy feet.

‒»» «‹‹

NEW POEMS

FROM *Part II*

‒»» «‹‹

ARCHAÏSCHER TORSO APOLLOS

Wir kannten nicht sein unerhörtes Haupt,
darin die Augenäpfel reiften. Aber
sein Torso glüht noch wie ein Kandelaber,
in dem sein Schauen, nur zurückgeschraubt,

sich hält und glänzt. Sonst könnte nicht der Bug
der Brust dich blenden, und im leisen Drehen
der Lenden könnte nicht ein Lächeln gehen
zu jener Mitte, die die Zeugung trug.

Sonst stünde dieser Stein entstellt und kurz
unter der Schultern durchsichtigem Sturz
und flimmerte nicht so wie Raubtierfelle

und bräche nicht aus allen seinen Rändern
aus wie ein Stern: denn da ist keine Stelle,
die dich nicht sieht. Du musst dein Leben ändern.

ARCHAIC TORSO OF APOLLO

We did not know his legendary head,
in which the eyeballs ripened. But
his torso still glows like a candelabrum
in which his gaze, only turned low,

holds and gleams. Else could not the curve
of the breast blind you, nor in the slight turn
of the loins could a smile be running
to that middle, which carried procreation.

Else would this stone be standing maimed and short
under the shoulders' translucent plunge
nor flimmering like the fell of beasts of prey

nor breaking out of all its contours
like a star: for there is no place
that does not see you. You must change your life.

ADAM

Staunend steht er an der Kathedrale
steilem Aufstieg, nah der Fensterrose,
wie erschreckt von der Apotheose,
welche wuchs und ihn mit einem Male

niederstellte über die und die.
Und er ragt und freut sich seiner Dauer,
schlicht entschlossen; als der Ackerbauer
der begann und der nicht wusste, wie

aus dem fertig-vollen Garten Eden
einen Ausweg in die neue Erde
finden. Gott war schwer zu überreden;

und er drohte ihm, statt zu gewähren,
immer wieder, dass er sterben werde.
Doch der Mensch bestand: sie wird gebären.

ADAM

Marveling he stands on the cathedral's
steep ascent, close to the rose window,
as though frightened at the apotheosis
which grew and all at once

set him down over these and these.
And straight he stands and glad of his endurance,
simply determined; as the husbandman
who began and who knew not how

from the garden of Eden finished-full
to find a way out into
the new earth. God was hard to persuade;

and threatened him, instead of acceding,
ever and again, that he would die.
Yet man persisted: she will bring forth.

EVA

Einfach steht sie an der Kathedrale
grossem Aufstieg, nah der Fensterrose,
mit dem Apfel in der Apfelpose,
schuldlos-schuldig ein für alle Male

an dem Wachsenden, das sie gebar,
seit sie aus dem Kreis der Ewigkeiten
liebend fortging, um sich durchzustreiten
durch die Erde, wie ein junges Jahr.

Ach, sie hätte gern in jenem Lande
noch ein wenig weilen mögen, achtend
auf der Tiere Eintracht und Verstand.

Doch da sie den Mann entschlossen fand,
ging sie mit ihm, nach dem Tode trachtend,
und sie hatte Gott noch kaum gekannt.

EVE

Simply she stands on the cathedral's
great ascent, close to the rose window,
with the apple in the apple-pose,
guiltless-guilty once and for all

of the growing she gave birth to
since from the circle of eternities
loving she went forth, to struggle through
her way throughout the earth like a young year.

Ah, gladly yet a little in that land
would she have lingered, heeding the harmony
and understanding of the animals.

But since she found the man determined,
she went with him, aspiring after death,
and she had as yet hardly known God.

LIED VOM MEER

CAPRI, PICCOLA MARINA

Uraltes Wehn vom Meer,
Meerwind bei Nacht:
du kommst zu keinem her;
wenn einer wacht,
so muss er sehn, wie er
dich übersteht:
uraltes Wehn vom Meer,
welches weht
nur wie für Urgestein,
lauter Raum
reissend von weit herein.

O wie fühlt dich ein
treibender Feigenbaum
oben im Mondenschein.

SONG OF THE SEA

CAPRI, PICCOLA MARINA

Age-old waft from the sea,
sea-wind by night:
you come to no one hither;
if someone wakes,
then he must see how he
endures against you:
age-old waft from the sea,
which wafts
alone as for primeval rock,
tearing sheer space
in with it from afar.

O how a burgeoning
fig tree feels you
above in the moonlight.

DIE LIEBENDE

Das ist mein Fenster. Eben
bin ich so sanft erwacht.
Ich dachte, ich würde schweben.
Bis wohin reicht mein Leben,
und wo beginnt die Nacht?

Ich könnte meinen, alles
wäre noch ich ringsum;
durchsichtig wie eines Kristalles
Tiefe, verdunkelt, stumm.

Ich könnte auch noch die Sterne
fassen in mir; so gross
scheint mir mein Herz; so gerne
liess es ihn wieder los,

den ich vielleicht zu lieben,
vielleicht zu halten begann.
Fremd wie niebeschrieben
sieht mich mein Schicksal an.

Was bin ich unter diese
Unendlichkeit gelegt,
duftend wie eine Wiese,
hin und her bewegt,

rufend zugleich und bange,
dass einer den Ruf vernimmt,
und zum Untergange
in einem andern bestimmt.

GIRL IN LOVE

That is my window. Just now
did I so softly wake.
I thought I was about to soar.
To where does my life reach,
and where does the night begin?

I could believe everything
round about was still I;
transparent as a crystal's
depth, darkened, silent.

I could hold even the stars
in me too; so big
my heart seems to me; so gladly
would it let him go again

whom I began perhaps
to love, perhaps to hold.
Strange as if never written
my fate is looking at me.

Why am I laid under
this infinity,
fragrant as a meadow,
swayed to and fro,

calling withal and fearing
lest one perceive the call,
and destined to extinction
in another.

SCHLAFLIED

Einmal, wenn ich dich verlier,
wirst du schlafen können, ohne
dass ich wie eine Lindenkrone
mich verflüstre über dir?

Ohne dass ich hier wache und
Worte, beinah wie Augenlider,
auf deine Brüste, auf deine Glieder
niederlege, auf deinen Mund?

Ohne dass ich dich verschliess
und dich allein mit Deinem lasse,
wie einen Garten mit einer Masse
von Melissen und Sternanis?

SLUMBERSONG

Some day, when I lose you,
will you be able to sleep without
my whispering myself away
like a linden's crown above you?

Without my waking here and laying down
words, almost like eyelids,
upon your breasts, upon your limbs,
upon your mouth?

Without my closing you and leaving
you alone with what is yours,
like a garden with a mass
of melissas and star-anise?

※

THE LIFE OF THE VIRGIN MARY

ζάλην ἔνδοθεν ἔχων

※

GEBURT MARIÄ

O was muss es die Engel gekostet haben,
nicht aufzusingen plötzlich, wie man aufweint,
da sie doch wussten: in dieser Nacht wird dem Knaben
die Mutter geboren, dem Einen, der bald erscheint.

Schwingend verschwiegen sie sich und zeigten die Richtung,
wo, allein, das Gehöft lag des Joachim,
ach, sie fühlten in sich und im Raum die reine Verdichtung,
aber es durfte keiner nieder zu ihm.

Denn die beiden waren schon so ausser sich vor Getue.
Eine Nachbarin kam und klugte und wusste nicht wie,
und der Alte, vorsichtig, ging und verhielt das Gemuhe
einer dunkelen Kuh. Denn so war es noch nie.

BIRTH OF MARY

O what must it have cost the angels
not suddenly to burst into song, as one bursts into tears,
since indeed they knew: on this night the mother is being
born to the boy, the One, who shall soon appear.

Soaring they held themselves silent and showed the direction
where, alone, Joachim's farm lay;
ah, they felt in themselves and in space the pure precipitation,
but none might go down to him.

For the two were already quite beside themselves with ado.
A neighbor-woman came and played wise and did not know how,
and the old man, carefully, went and withheld the mooing
of a dark cow. For so it had never yet been.

DIE DARSTELLUNG MARIÄ IM TEMPEL

Um zu begreifen wie sie damals war,
musst du dich erst an eine Stelle rufen,
wo Säulen in dir wirken; wo du Stufen
nachfühlen kannst; wo Bogen voll Gefahr
den Abgrund eines Raumes überbrücken,
der in dir blieb, weil er aus solchen Stücken
getürmt war, dass du sie nicht mehr aus dir
ausheben kannst: du rissest dich denn ein.
Bist du so weit, ist alles in dir Stein,
Wand, Aufgang, Durchblick, Wölbung—, so probier,
den grossen Vorhang, den du vor dir hast,
ein wenig wegzuzerrn mit beiden Händen:
Da glänzt es von ganz hohen Gegenständen
und übertrifft dir Atem und Getast.
Hinauf, hinab, Palast sieht auf Palast,
Geländer strömen breiter aus Geländern
und tauchen oben auf an solchen Rändern,
dass dich, wie du sie siehst, der Schwindel fasst.
Dabei macht ein Gewölk aus Räucherständern
die Nähe trüb; aber das Fernste zielt
in dich hinein mit seinen graden Strahlen—,
und wenn jetzt Schein aus klaren Flammenschalen
auf langsam nahenden Gewändern spielt:
wie hältst du's aus?

Sie aber kam und hob
den Blick, um dieses alles anzuschauen.
(Ein Kind, ein kleines Mädchen zwischen Frauen.)
Dann stieg sie ruhig, voller Selbstvertrauen,

THE PRESENTATION OF MARY IN THE TEMPLE

To understand what she was like at that time,
you must first summon yourself to a place
where columns work in you; where you can follow
the feel of steps; where arches full of danger
bridge over the chasm of a space
that stayed in you because it was piled up
of such pieces, you can no longer lift them
out of you, lest you tear yourself down in ruins.
When you have got so far that all in you is stone,
wall, stairway, perspective, vaulting—, then try
with both hands to drag away a little
the great curtain that you have before you:
A radiance shines out from very high things
and overpowers your breath and touch.
Upward, downward, palace looks on palace,
balustrades stream broader out of balustrades
and reappear above along such edges
that, as you see them, dizziness grips you.
Meanwhile a cloud of haze from incense-burners
makes the foreground misty; but the farthest distance
shoots into you with its straight rays—,
and if now luster from clear bowls of flame
plays upon slowly approaching robes:
how can you bear it?

She, though, came and raised
her eyes to look upon all this.
(A child, a little girl between women.)
Then she mounted quietly, full of self-confidence,

dem Aufwand zu, der sich verwöhnt verschob:
So sehr war alles, was die Menschen bauen,
schon überwogen von dem Lob

in ihrem Herzen. Von der Lust
sich hinzugeben an die innern Zeichen:
Die Eltern meinten, sie hinaufzureichen,
der Drohende mit der Juwelenbrust
empfing sie scheinbar: Doch sie ging durch alle,
klein wie sie war, aus jeder Hand hinaus
und in ihr Los, das, höher als die Halle,
schon fertig war, und schwerer als das Haus.

towards the pomp that fastidiously made way:
So much was everything that mankind builds
already overwhelmed by the praise

in her heart. By her desire
to yield herself to the inner signs:
Her parents thought they were handing her up,
the threatening one with the bejeweled breast
received her it seemed: Yet she went through them all,
small as she was, forth out of every hand
and into her destiny, which, higher than the hall,
was prepared already, and heavier than the house.

MARIÄ VERKÜNDIGUNG

Nicht dass ein Engel eintrat (das erkenn),
erschreckte sie. So wenig andre, wenn
ein Sonnenstrahl oder der Mond bei Nacht
in ihrem Zimmer sich zu schaffen macht,
auffahren—, pflegte sie an der Gestalt,
in der ein Engel ging, sich zu entrüsten;
sie ahnte kaum dass dieser Aufenthalt
mühsam für Engel ist. (O wenn wir wüssten,
wie rein sie war. Hat eine Hirschkuh nicht,
die, liegend, einmal sie im Wald eräugte,
sich so in sie versehn, dass sich in ihr,
ganz ohne Paarigen, das Einhorn zeugte,
das Tier aus Licht, das reine Tier—.)
Nicht, dass er eintrat, aber dass er dicht,
der Engel, eines Jünglings Angesicht
so zu ihr neigte, dass sein Blick und der
mit dem sie aufsah, so zusammenschlugen,
als wäre draussen plötzlich alles leer
und, was Millionen schauten, trieben, trugen,
hineingedrängt in sie: nur sie und er;
Schaun und Geschautes, Aug und Augenweide
sonst nirgends als an dieser Stelle—: sieh,
dieses erschreckt. Und sie erschraken beide.

Dann sang der Engel seine Melodie.

ANNUNCIATION TO MARY

Not that an angel entered (mark this)
was she startled. Little as others start
when a ray of sun or the moon by night
busies itself about their room,
would she have been disturbed by the shape
in which an angel went;
she scarcely guessed that this sojourn
is irksome for angels. (O if we knew
how pure she was. Did not a hind, that,
recumbent, once espied her in the wood,
so lose itself in looking, that in it,
quite without pairing, the unicorn begot itself,
the creature of light, the pure creature—.)
Not that he entered, but that he,
the angel, so bent close to her
a youth's face that his gaze and that
with which she looked up struck together,
as though outside it were suddenly all empty
and what millions saw, did, bore,
were crowded into them: just she and he;
seeing and what is seen, eye and eye's delight
nowhere else save at this spot—: lo,
this is startling. And they were startled both.

Then the angel sang his melody.

MARIÄ HEIMSUCHUNG

Noch erging sie's leicht im Anbeginne,
doch im Steigen manchmal ward sie schon
ihres wunderbaren Leibes inne,—
und dann stand sie, atmend, auf den hohn

Judenbergen. Aber nicht das Land,
ihre Fülle war um sie gebreitet;
gehend fühlte sie: man überschreitet
nie die Grösse, die sie jetzt empfand.

Und es drängte sie, die Hand zu legen
auf den andern Leib, der weiter war.
Und die Frauen schwankten sich entgegen
und berührten sich Gewand und Haar.

Jede, voll von ihrem Heiligtume,
schützte sich mit der Gevatterin.
Ach der Heiland in ihr war noch Blume,
doch den Täufer in dem Schoos der Muhme
riss die Freude schon zum Hüpfen hin.

VISITATION OF THE VIRGIN

She still walked easily at first,
but in climbing sometimes she was already
aware of her wonderful body,—
and then she stood, breathing, upon the high

hills of Judea. But not the land,
her abundance was spread about her;
as she went she felt one never could exceed
the bigness she was feeling now.

And she craved to lay her hand
on the other body, that was further on.
And the women swayed towards one another
and touched each other's dress and hair.

Each, filled with her holy possession,
sought protection of her kinswoman.
Ah, the Savior in her was still flower,
though the Baptist in her cousin's womb
already leapt in transports of joy.

ARGWOHN JOSEPHS

Und der Engel sprach und gab sich Müh
an dem Mann, der seine Fäuste ballte:
Aber siehst du nicht an jeder Falte,
dass sie kühl ist wie die Gottesfrüh.

Doch der andre sah ihn finster an,
murmelnd nur: Was hat sie so verwandelt?
Doch da schrie der Engel: Zimmermann,
merkst du's noch nicht, dass der Herrgott handelt?

Weil du Bretter machst, in deinem Stolze,
willst du wirklich den zur Rede stelln,
der bescheiden aus dem gleichen Holze
Blätter treiben macht und Knospen schwelln?

Er begriff. Und wie er jetzt die Blicke
recht erschrocken, zu dem Engel hob,
war der fort. Da schob er seine dicke
Mütze langsam ab. Dann sang er lob.

JOSEPH'S SUSPICION

And the angel spoke and made an effort
with the man, who clenched his fists:
But dost thou not see by every fold
that she is cool as God's early day.

Yet the other looked somberly at him,
murmuring only: What has changed her so?
But at that the angel cried: Carpenter,
dost thou not yet see that the Lord God is acting?

Because thou makest boards, in thy pride,
wouldst thou really call him to account
who modestly out of the same wood
makes leaves burgeon and buds swell?

He understood. And as he now raised his eyes
very frightened, to the angel,
he was gone. He pushed his heavy
cap slowly off. Then he sang praise.

VERKÜNDIGUNG ÜBER DEN HIRTEN

Seht auf, ihr Männer. Männer dort am Feuer,
die ihr den grenzenlosen Himmel kennt,
Sterndeuter, hierher! Seht, ich bin ein neuer
steigender Stern. Mein ganzes Wesen brennt
und strahlt so stark und ist so ungeheuer
voll Licht, dass mir das tiefe Firmament
nicht mehr genügt. Lasst meinen Glanz hinein
in euer Dasein: o, die dunklen Blicke,
die dunklen Herzen, nächtige Geschicke,
die euch erfüllen. Hirten, wie allein
bin ich in euch. Auf einmal wird mir Raum.
Stauntet ihr nicht: der grosse Brotfruchtbaum
warf einen Schatten. Ja, das kam von mir.
Ihr Unerschrockenen, o wüsstet ihr,
wie jetzt auf eurem schauenden Gesichte
die Zukunft scheint. In diesem starken Lichte
wird viel geschehen. Euch vertrau ichs, denn
ihr seid verschwiegen; euch Gradgläubigen
redet hier alles. Glut und Regen spricht,
der Vögel Zug, der Wind und was ihr seid,
keins überwiegt und wächst zur Eitelkeit
sich mästend an. Ihr haltet nicht
die Dinge auf im Zwischenraum der Brust,
um sie zu quälen. So wie seine Lust
durch einen Engel strömt, so treibt durch euch
das Irdische. Und wenn ein Dorngesträuch
aufflammte plötzlich, dürfte noch aus ihm
der Ewige euch rufen, Cherubim,

ANNUNCIATION OVER THE SHEPHERDS

Look up, you men. Men there at the fire,
you who know the boundless heaven,
star-readers, this way! See, I am a new
rising star. My whole being burns
and shines so strongly and is so immensely
full of light that the deep firmament
no longer suffices me. Let my radiance
into your existence: oh, the dark looks,
the dark hearts, destinies like night,
that fill you. Shepherds, how alone
I am in you. Suddenly I have room.
Did you not marvel: the great breadfruit tree
threw a shadow. Yes, that came from me.
You fearless ones, oh if you knew
how upon your gazing vision now
the future shines. In this strong light
much will happen. To you I confide it, for
you are discreet; to you honest believers
all things here speak. Fire and rain speaks,
passage of birds, the wind and what you are,
none prevails and grows to vanity
glutting itself. You do not hold things back
in the breast's interval
in order to torment them. As his ecstasy
streams through an angel, so the earthly
goes through you. And should a thornbush
suddenly flame up, out of which even
the Lord might call you; cherubim,

wenn sie geruhten neben eurer Herde
einherzuschreiten, wunderten euch nicht:
ihr stürztet euch auf euer Angesicht,
betetet an und nenntet dies die Erde.

Doch dieses war. Nun soll ein neues sein,
von dem der Erdkreis ringender sich weitet.
Was ist ein Dörnicht uns: Gott fühlt sich ein
in einer Jungfrau Schooss. Ich bin der Schein
von ihrer Innigkeit, der euch geleitet.

if they deigned to walk alongside
your herd, would not surprise you:
you would cast yourselves upon your faces,
worship and call this the earth.

But this has been. Now shall a new thing be,
by which the world shall spread in wider circles.
What is a thornbush to us: God feels his way
into a virgin's womb. I am the shine
of her lovingness, that goes with you.

GEBURT CHRISTI

Hättest du der Einfalt nicht, wie sollte
dir geschehn, was jetzt die Nacht erhellt?
Sieh, der Gott, der über Völker grollte,
macht sich mild und kommt in dir zur Welt.

Hast du dir ihn grösser vorgestellt?

Was ist Grösse? Quer durch alle Masse,
die er durchstreicht, geht sein grades Los.
Selbst ein Stern hat keine solche Strasse,
siehst du, diese Könige sind gross,

und sie schleppen dir vor deinen Schooss

Schätze, die sie für die grössten halten,
und du staunst vielleicht bei dieser Gift—:
aber schau in deines Tuches Falten,
wie er jetzt schon alles übertrifft.

Aller Amber, den man weit verschifft,
jeder Goldschmuck und das Luftgewürze,
das sich trübend in die Sinne streut:
alles dieses war von rascher Kürze,
und am Ende hat man es bereut.

Aber (du wirst sehen): Er erfreut.

BIRTH OF CHRIST

Hadst thou not simplicity, how should
that happen to thee which now lights up the night?
See, the God who rumbled over nations
makes himself mild and in thee comes into the world.

Hadst thou imagined him greater?

What is greatness? Right through all measures
that he crosses goes his straight destiny.
Even a star has no such path,
see thou, these kings are great,

and they drag before thy lap

treasures that they hold to be the greatest,
and thou art perhaps astonished at this gift—:
but look into the folds of thy shawl,
how even now he has exceeded all.

All amber that one ships afar,
all ornament of gold and the aromatic spice
that spreads blurringly in the senses:
all this was of rapid brevity,
and who knows but one has regretted it.

But (thou wilt see): He brings joy.

RAST AUF DER FLUCHT IN ÄGYPTEN

Diese, die noch eben atemlos
flohen mitten aus dem Kindermorden:
o, wie waren sie unmerklich gross
über ihrer Wanderschaft geworden.

Kaum noch dass im scheuen Rückwärtsschauen
ihres Schreckens Not zergangen war,
und schon brachten sie auf ihrem grauen
Maultier ganze Städte in Gefahr;

denn sowie sie, klein im grossen Land,
—fast ein Nichts—den starken Tempeln nahten,
platzten alle Götzen wie verraten
und verloren völlig den Verstand.

Ist es denkbar, dass von ihrem Gange
alles so verzweifelt sich erbost?
Und sie wurden vor sich selber bange,
nur das Kind war namenlos getrost.

Immerhin, sie mussten sich darüber
eine Weile setzen. Doch da ging—
sieh: der Baum, der still sie überhing,
wie ein Dienender zu ihnen über:

er verneigte sich. Derselbe Baum,
dessen Kränze toten Pharaonen
für das Ewige die Stirnen schonen,
neigte sich. Er fühlte neue Kronen
blühen. Und sie sassen wie im Traum.

REST ON THE FLIGHT INTO EGYPT

These, who even now fled breathless
from amid the slaughter of children:
oh, how they had imperceptibly grown
through their wandering.

Scarcely yet in the timid looking backward
had their fright's extremity dissolved,
and already they were bringing on their gray
mule whole cities into danger;

for as they, small in the great land,
—almost a nothing—neared the strong temples,
all the idols crashed as though betrayed
and entirely lost their senses.

Is it conceivable that at their passing
everything grew so desperately enraged?
And they became afraid of themselves,
only the child was namelessly at ease.

And yet, because of this they had
to sit awhile. But there—see:
the tree that hung motionless above them
went over to them like one serving:

it bowed. The same tree,
whose garlands for eternity
shelter dead Pharaohs' brows,
bowed. It felt new crowns
blooming. And they sat as in a dream.

VON DER HOCHZEIT ZU KANA

Konnte sie denn anders, als auf ihn
stolz sein, der ihr Schlichtestes verschönte?
War nicht selbst die hohe, grossgewöhnte
Nacht wie ausser sich, da er erschien?

Ging nicht auch, dass er sich einst verloren,
unerhört zu seiner Glorie aus?
Hatten nicht die weisesten die Ohren
mit dem Mund vertauscht? Und war das Haus

nicht wie neu von seiner Stimme? Ach,
sicher hatte sie zu hundert Malen
ihre Freude an ihm auszustrahlen
sich verwehrt. Sie ging ihm staunend nach.

Aber da bei jenem Hochzeitsfeste,
als es unversehens an Wein gebrach,—
sah sie hin und bat um eine Geste
und begriff nicht, dass er widersprach.

Und dann tat ers. Sie verstand es später,
wie sie ihn in seinen Weg gedrängt:
denn jetzt war er wirklich Wundertäter,
und das ganze Opfer war verhängt,

unaufhaltsam. Ja, es stand geschrieben.
Aber war es damals schon bereit?
Sie: sie hatte es herbeigetrieben

OF THE MARRIAGE AT CANA

Could she do otherwise than be proud
of him who made the simplest beautiful to her?
Was not even the lofty, large-accustomed
night as if beside itself when he appeared?

Did not also his once having lost himself
incredibly redound to his glory?
Had not the wisest exchanged ears
for mouths? And was not the house

as new at his voice? Ah,
surely she had hundreds of times restrained
herself from radiating her delight
in him. She followed him amazed.

But there at that wedding feast,
when unexpectedly there was no wine,—
she looked across and begged him for a gesture
and did not understand that he protested.

And then he did it. She realized later
how she had pressed him into his way:
for now he really was performing miracles,
and the whole sacrifice was decreed,

irresistibly. Yes, it was written.
But was it already then prepared?
She: she had brought it on

in der Blindheit ihrer Eitelkeit.

An dem Tisch voll Früchten und Gemüsen
freute sie sich mit und sah nicht ein,
dass das Wasser ihrer Tränendrüsen
Blut geworden war mit diesem Wein.

in the blindness of her vanity.

At the table full of fruits and vegetables
she rejoiced with the rest and did not understand
that the water of her tear-glands
had turned to blood with this wine.

VOR DER PASSION

O hast du dies gewollt, du hättest nicht
durch eines Weibes Leib entspringen dürfen:
Heilande muss man in den Bergen schürfen,
wo man das Harte aus dem Harten bricht.

Tut dirs nicht selber leid, dein liebes Tal
so zu verwüsten? Siehe meine Schwäche;
ich habe nichts als Milch- und Tränenbäche,
und du warst immer in der Überzahl.

Mit solchem Aufwand wardst du mir verheissen.
Was tratst du nicht gleich wild aus mir hinaus?
Wenn du nur Tiger brauchst, dich zu zerreissen,
warum erzog man mich im Frauenhaus,

ein weiches reines Kleid für dich zu weben,
darin nicht einmal die geringste Spur
von Naht dich drückt—: so war mein ganzes Leben,
und jetzt verkehrst du plötzlich die Natur.

BEFORE THE PASSION

O if you wanted this you should not have been
allowed to spring forth through a woman's body:
saviors should be quarried in the mountains,
where the hard is broken from the hard.

Are you yourself not sorry so to lay waste
your beloved valley? See my weakness:
I have nothing but brooks of milk and tears,
and you were always in excess.

With such lavishness were you promised me.
Why not at once have gone wildly out of me?
If you only need tigers to tear you to pieces,
why did they raise me in the women's house

to weave a soft clean dress for you,
in which not even the slightest trace of a seam
presses against you—: my whole life was like that,
and now you suddenly turn Nature upside down.

PIETÀ

Jetzt wird mein Elend voll, und namenlos
erfüllt es mich. Ich starre, wie des Steins
Inneres starrt.
Hart wie ich bin, weiss ich nur Eins:
Du wurdest gross—
. . . und wurdest gross,
um als zu grosser Schmerz
ganz über meines Herzens Fassung
hinauszustehn.
Jetzt liegst du quer durch meinen Schooss,
jetzt kann ich dich nicht mehr
gebären.

PIETÀ

Now is my misery full, and namelessly
it fills me. I am stark, as the stone's
inside is stark.
Hard as I am, I know but one thing:
You grew—
. . . and grew
in order to stand forth
as too great pain
quite beyond my heart's grasping.
Now you are lying straight across my lap,
now I can no longer
give you birth.

STILLUNG MARIÄ MIT DEM
AUFERSTANDENEN

Was sie damals empfanden: ist es nicht
vor allen Geheimnissen süss
und immer noch irdisch:
da er, ein wenig blass noch vom Grab,
erleichtert zu ihr trat:
an allen Stellen erstanden.
O zu ihr zuerst. Wie waren sie da
unaussprechlich in Heilung.
Ja, sie heilten, das wars. Sie hatten nicht nötig,
sich stark zu berühren.
Er legte ihr eine Sekunde
kaum seine nächstens
ewige Hand an die frauliche Schulter.
Und sie begannen
still wie die Bäume im Frühling,
unendlich zugleich,
diese Jahreszeit
ihres äussersten Umgangs.

CONSOLATION OF MARY WITH
CHRIST ARISEN

What they felt then: is it not
before all secrets sweet
and yet still earthly:
as he, a little pale still from the grave,
relieved stepped up to her:
at every point arisen.
O to her first. How were they then
inexpressibly being healed.
Yes, they were healing, that was it. They had no need
firmly to touch each other.
He laid for a second
scarcely his soon to be
eternal hand to her womanly shoulder.
And they began,
still as the trees in Spring,
infinitely together,
this season
of their ultimate communing.

VOM TODE MARIÄ

(DREI STÜCKE)

I

Derselbe grosse Engel, welcher einst
ihr der Gebärung Botschaft niederbrachte,
stand da, abwartend, dass sie ihn beachte,
und sprach: Jetzt wird es Zeit, dass du erscheinst.
Und sie erschrak wie damals und erwies
sich wieder als die Magd, ihn tief bejahend.
Er aber strahlte, und unendlich nahend,
schwand er wie in ihr Angesicht—und hiess
die weithin ausgegangenen Bekehrer
zusammenkommen in das Haus am Hang,
das Haus des Abendmahls. Sie kamen schwerer
und traten bange ein: Da lag, entlang
die schmale Bettstatt, die in Untergang
und Auserwählung rätselhaft Getauchte,
ganz unversehrt, wie eine Ungebrauchte,
und achtete auf englischen Gesang.
Nun da sie alle hinter ihren Kerzen
abwarten sah, riss sie vom Übermass
der Stimmen sich und schenckte noch von Herzen
die beiden Kleider fort, die sie besass,
und hob ihr Antlitz auf zu dem und dem . . .
(o Ursprung namenloser Tränen-Bäche).

Sie aber legte sich in ihre Schwäche

OF THE DEATH OF MARY

(THREE PIECES)

I

The same great angel who had once
brought her down the message of her bearing,
stood there, waiting for her to notice him,
and spoke: Now it is time that thou appear.
And she was startled as before and showed
herself the maid again, deeply confirming him.
But he shone, and infinitely nearing,
vanished as it were into her face—
and bade the evangelists gone forth afar
to come together in the house on the slope,
the house of the last supper. They came more heavily
and entered fearfully: There, along
the narrow bed, she lay, in her passing
and election mysteriously immersed,
quite inviolate, like one unused,
heeding angelic song.
Now that she saw them all waiting behind
their candles, she tore herself from the excess
of voices and with all her heart yet gave
away the two dresses she possessed,
and lifted her face to this one and to that . . .
(o source of nameless brooks of tears).

But she lay back in her weakness

und zog die Himmel an Jerusalem
so nah heran, dass ihre Seele nur,
austretend, sich ein wenig strecken musste:
schon hob er sie, der alles von ihr wusste,
hinein in ihre göttliche Natur.

II

Wer hat bedacht, dass bis zu ihrem Kommen
der viele Himmel unvollständig war?
Der Auferstandene hat Platz genommen,
doch nebem ihm, durch vierundzwanzig Jahr,
war leer der Sitz. Und sie begannen schon
sich an die reine Lücke zu gewöhnen,
die wie verheilt war, denn mit seinem schönen
Hinüberscheinen füllte sie der Sohn.

So ging auch sie, die in die Himmel trat,
nicht auf ihn zu, so sehr es sie verlangte;
dort war kein Platz, nur Er war dort und prangte
mit einer Strahlung, die ihr wehe tat.
Doch da sie jetzt, die rührende Gestalt,
sich zu den neuen Seligen gesellte
und unauffällig, licht zu licht, sich stellte,
da brach aus ihrem Sein ein Hinterhalt

and drew the heavens so close to Jerusalem
that her soul, departing, needed but
to stretch itself a little:
already he, who knew everything about her,
was lifting her into her divine nature.

II

Who has considered that until her coming
the manifold heaven was incomplete?
The resurrected one had taken his place,
but next him, throughout four and twenty years,
the seat was empty. And already they began
to grow accustomed to the clean gap that was
as if healed over, for with his beautiful
overspreading shine the son filled it.

So even she, entering the heavens, went
not towards him, much as she longed to. There was
no room there, only He was there, resplendent
with a radiance that hurt her.
Yet as she now, that moving figure,
joined the newly blessed and took her place,
inconspicuous, light to light,
there broke out of her being a withheld store

von solchem Glanz, dass der von ihr erhellte
Engel geblendet aufschrie: Wer ist die?
Ein Staunen war. Dann sahn sie alle, wie
Gott-Vater oben unsern Herrn verhielt,
so dass von milder Dämmerung umspielt,
die leere Stelle wie ein wenig Leid
sich zeigte, eine Spur von Einsamkeit,
wie etwas, was er noch ertrug, ein Rest
irdischer Zeit, ein trockenes Gebrest—.
Man sah nach ihr: sie schaute ängstlich hin,
weit vorgeneigt, als fühlte sie: ich bin
sein längster Schmerz—: und stürzte plötzlich vor.
Die Engel aber nahmen sie zu sich
und stützten sie und sangen seliglich
und trugen sie das letzte Stück empor.

III

Doch vor dem Apostel Thomas, der
kam, da es zu spät war, trat der schnelle
längst darauf gefasste Engel her
und befahl an der Begräbnisstelle:

Dräng den Stein beiseite. Willst du wissen,
wo die ist, die dir das Herz bewegt:

of such glory, that the angel lighted up
by her cried out dazzled: Who is she?
Amazement reigned. Then they all saw how
above God the Father withheld our Lord
so that, with mild twilight playing round it,
the empty place showed like a bit of sorrow,
a trace of loneliness, like something
he was still enduring, a residue
of earthly time, a dried-up canker—.
They looked towards her: she was watching anxiously,
leaning far out, as though she felt: *I* am
his longest pain—: and suddenly plunged forward.
But the angels took her to themselves
and supported her and sang beatifically
and carried her the last stretch aloft.

III

But before the Apostle Thomas, who
came when it was too late, stepped the swift
angel, long since prepared for this,
and commanded at the burial-place:

Push the stone aside. Wouldst thou know
where she is who has moved thy heart:

Sieh: sie ward wie ein Lavendelkissen
eine Weile da hineingelegt,

dass die Erde künftig nach ihr rieche
in den Falten wie ein feines Tuch.
Alles Tote (fühlst du), alles Sieche
ist betäubt von ihrem Wohlgeruch.

Schau den Leinwand: wo ist eine Bleiche,
wo er blendend wird und geht nicht ein?
Dieses Licht aus dieser reinen Leiche
war ihm klärender als Sonnenschein.

Staunst du nicht, wie sanft sie ihm entging?
Fast als wär sie's noch, nichts ist verschoben.
Doch die Himmel sind erschüttert oben:
Mann, knie hin und sieh mir nach und sing.

See: like a cushion of lavender
she was laid in there a while,

that in future the earth smell of her
in its folds like a fine napkin.
Everything dead (thou feelest), everything sickly
is numbed with her good fragrance.

Behold the winding-sheet: where is a bleaching place
where it would grow dazzling and not shrink?
This light from this pure corpse
was more clarifying to it than sunshine.

Are you not astonished, how gently she went from it?
Almost as though it were still she, nothing is displaced.
Yet the heavens are shaken above:
Man, kneel down, look after me and sing.

NOTES

Rilke was born in Prague on December 4, 1875, and died at Val-Mont, near Glion, Switzerland, on December 29, 1926.

FIRST POEMS

IN considering the publication of a selection from his older and newer poems, Rilke expressed himself (to Stefan Zweig, February 14, 1907) as not knowing "what place those youthful works may lay claim to and whether they are entitled to any at all. To me they have always more shown their inadequacy; I do not repudiate them, but it seems to me that I so very much have one thing—and again and again this one thing—to say, that they have simply been replaced through the better and more mature expression and so anyway merely represent something like provisional things that have survived over against what is definitive." When he had finally agreed to let Insel-Verlag publish the collection under this title (1913), he wrote Anton Kippenberg (January 15, 1912): "You will be doing me the greatest possible kindness if you will postpone the First Poems yet a little. Nowhere could I undertake the revision of whatever comes in question there better and more conscientiously than in a certain tower-room [at the Kippenbergs']: may I let the matter hang fire until I breathe that room's beneficence again and meanwhile just lay everything together—? (hélas, it will be only a little pile of well-meant papers anyhow.)" The *First Poems* nevertheless found their place in the *Collected Works* (1927) as planned with Rilke's approval.

Advent, from which the present verses are selected, was first published in 1898, as "Poems (Munich 1896/97) to my good father under the Christmas tree." Rilke wrote Ellen Key (March 3, 1904) that she would miss nothing if she did not learn to know these poems. "My powers were so slight then, my feeling unripe and timid, and add to this that for all my first publications I always assembled the poorest and least personal of my experiments, because I could not bring my-self to hand over what I was really fond of; so naturally these became pitiful books (*erbärmliche Bücher*)."

Of the nine poems translated here, the first five belong in a section entitled "Gifts to Various Friends (*Gaben an verschiedene Freunde*)," but the names of the individuals to whom they were dedicated have not been carried over into subsequent editions. About *"Peacock-feather . . ."* however, Rilke wrote (November 12, 1901) to his wife's young brother, Helmuth Westhoff, to whom he enclosed a copy of the poem, that it had been written "some five years ago . . . in the city of Munich, where in October they have something rather like your free market. A large meadow full of show booths. And while the other people were going around and laughing and teasing each other and trying to reach and tickle each other with long peacockfeathers (which they found great fun), I went around alone with my peacock-feather, which was much too proud to tickle anybody, and the longer I carried it around with me, the more did the slenderness of its form occupy me, how it swayed on its elastic stalk, and the beauty of its head, out of which the 'peacockeye' looked at me dark and secretly. I felt as though I were seeing such a feather for the first time, and it seemed to me to contain a whole profusion of beauties which no one noticed but I. And out of this feeling the little poem came into being, which I dedicated at that time to a dear friend, a painter [Emil Or-lik], of whom I knew that he too loved peacockfeathers. You may think what a peacockfeather means to a painter, who has a quite dif-ferent, much closer relationship to colors than we, how much he can learn from it and how much pleasure the harmony in the variety and the multitude of colors, all together there upon such a little spot, can give him.

"But do you know what was to me the main thing about it: that I once more saw that most people hold a thing in their hands in order to do something silly with it (as for example tickling each other with peacockfeathers), instead of looking well at each thing and instead of asking each thing about the beauty it possesses. So it comes that most people do not know at all how beautiful the world is and how much glory is manifest in the smallest things, in some flower, a stone, the bark of a tree, or a birchleaf. Grown people, who have affairs and cares and torment themselves with a lot of trifles, gradually lose entirely their eye for these riches, which children, if they are attentive and good, soon notice and love with all their heart. And yet it would be nicest if everybody would always remain in this respect like attentive and good children, simple and devout in feeling, and if they would not lose the ability to rejoice as sincerely in a birchleaf or a peacock's feather or the wings of a marsh heron as in a great mountain range or a magnificent palace. The small is no more small than the big—is big. A great and eternal beauty runs through the whole world, and it is justly spread over the small things and the large; for substantially and essentially there is no injustice upon the whole earth. This, dear Helmuth, all hangs together a little with the poem about the peacock-feather, in which I could but badly express what I meant. I was still very young then. But now I know it better with every year and am always better able to tell people that there is a great deal of beauty in the world—almost only beauty."

"Can you still play the old songs?" was not included in *Advent* until the *First Poems* were published in 1913.

THE BOOK OF PICTURES

UNDER this title there first appeared in 1902 forty-five poems, in an edition of 500 copies, dedicated to Gerhart Hauptmann "in affection and gratitude for *Michael Kramer.*" Rilke wrote Axel Juncker, the publisher (November 7, 1901): "This is an important moment for me, in which I send you the poems. This collection . . . is the most precious thing I have of these years, and in laying it in your hands I am gladly showing you a great confidence. . . . Read it . . . and try to feel how dear every line of it is to me." The edition with which we are familiar today is the much enlarged one (substantially as taken over by Insel-Verlag in 1913 and now in the *Collected Works*), pub-

lished in 1906, after Rilke's Paris experiences, his association with
Rodin, and many travels. Rilke spent considerable time and care in
the arranging of this edition, laying in the new poems not simply as
a body of later material but where he felt they belonged among the
older ones. He wrote his wife from Meudon on February 8, 1906: "I
write, I would like to say hundreds of letters, mornings for the Master
and afternoons for myself, and then if something is left over that is not
yet night, I hearken to my poems that still want to get into the Book
of Pictures. Slowly I listen to each one and let it die away even into
its furthest echo. Few will survive in the stillness in which I set them,
some will be altered, of many but a piece will remain and wait till,
some day perhaps, something comes and joins it. . . ."

Most of the earlier poems were presumably written at Schmargen-
dorf, near Berlin, where Rilke was living in 1899 and 1900, the period
covered by the published portions of the diary, or at Worpswede, the
artists' colony near Bremen, where he was a frequent visitor and where
he met Clara Westhoff, whom he married in 1901.

Prelude appears in the diary with the note: "written on an evening
walk in still, soft, darkening air, Dahlemer Strasse, February 24th
[1900]."

From an April is also entered in the diary, as written down on
"Friday, returning home through the first warm spring rain. April 6th,
1900."

Music and *The Angels* were written in 1900. (N.B. In the former,
das Viele would perhaps be more correctly translated as "the much,"
"muchness," "manifoldness"; but all these seeming heavy and prosy,
I have used "fullness," perhaps influenced in part by its two syllables
and the alliteration.)

Childhood was written in Paris in 1903, and is among the poems
chosen by Rilke in 1918, as representative of his best, to be included in
a privately printed volume of *Selected Poems.**

---

* For this information and for some of the dates I was unable to establish from
the *Letters,* I am indebted to Miss G. Craig Houston's notes, "Rilke's Buch der
Bilder," *Modern Language Review,* XXIX, 3, July 1934. The *Rilke Bibliographie*
compiled by Fritz Adolf Hünich (Insel, 1935) has also been helpful.

From a Childhood occurs as a diary entry of March 21, 1900, some variation in the closing lines showing that Rilke worked the poem over before publishing it.

The Boy: see note to *Childhood.*

The Last Supper was written in Milan in 1904. In a letter of July 3rd, Rilke describes the picture, which he had seen a few weeks before, as "supremely magnificent, painting that is near only to antique wall pictures, not to be compared with anything else; almost gone, almost only told by the deeply moved voice of someone invisible, and yet unspeakably there, presence, and in its core indestructible." (N.B. For *Schoten* I have used "sheaves," as a more usual English expression than the literal translation, "pods" or "cods.")

Initial (*Out of infinite yearnings*) belongs among the earlier poems.

To Say for Going to Sleep appears in the diary, November 14, 1900.

People by Night is part of a long diary entry entitled "Chanson Orpheline II," dated "Saturday, November 25th, 1899 (at night)."

The Neighbor was written in Paris (1903?).

Apprehension and *Lament* both occur in the diary, October 4, 1900.

Autumn Day and *Remembering* are presumably of later date, as they do not appear in the first edition. Their mood and imagery so strongly resemble those of Rilke's letters from Sweden in the autumn of 1904 that for lack of other more definite information one is tempted to wonder whether they were not written during or soon after his visit to that country.

Autumn: see note to *Childhood.*

On the Verge of Night appears in the diary, with slight variations, January 12, 1900.

Presentiment: see note to *Childhood.*

Evening, which Rilke also chose for the *Selected Poems,* was presumably written in Worpswede in 1900, although it is not included in the first edition.

Grave Hour appears in the diary, October 4, 1900, longer by two preceding verses.

Strophes, longer by a third verse, was written at the house of Heinrich Vogeler, the painter, at Worpswede in 1900.

Initial (*Simply give away your beauty*) dates from July 14, 1899.

Annunciation was written in Worpswede, 1900.

In the Certosa was written in Arco, where Rilke spent the first half of March 1899. (N.B. The *ihn* in the last line of the fourth verse may be considered ambiguous. Does it perhaps refer back to the young monk? My German advisers are not agreed on this point.)

The Singer Sings before a Child of Princes appears in the diary, October 3, 1900. On November 5th Rilke writes to Paula Becker, the "blond painter" of whom, as well as of Clara Westhoff, he was seeing a good deal at this time, and who later married the painter Otto Modersohn: "Shortly I will copy off the Song . . . and send it to you. It does not exist at all if you do not possess it,—just this, which so to speak began with you. In those evening hours"; and on January 13, 1901, his enthusiasm still runs high as he describes how he read the poem aloud all by himself, after they had spent the evening together, ". . . and followed the willing verse on and on and thought you still here, hearing and remembering. And it really was as though you were quite near—there, where my words come to an end, at the outermost edge of sound."

The Voices. Most—perhaps all—of the poems in this cycle were written in Paris, some earlier than others. On June 7, 1906, Rilke writes his wife: "I am particularly happy over three entirely new things, which, together with the Song of the Leper, are to make a group. You will love them too, I know, and quite *avant la lettre* as they are (entirely of today all three), I send them to you." They were the *Songs of the Dwarf, the Idiot,* and *the Blindman*. To his publisher he writes on June 12th that "this cycle broadens the book in one direction and will help it not to be given out henceforth as merely aesthetic in character." The *Songs of the Beggar* and *the Dwarf* were also chosen by Rilke for the *Selected Poems*. The *Song of the Widow* came out in *Deutsche Arbeit* for October 1906 over Rilke's signature and the date "Paris, Spring 1906." (N.B. Again an ambiguous pronoun, *seine* = his (verse 2, line 1), and again my German friends are not unanimous. Does it perhaps refer to life rather than to the husband? If so, read "its.")

Closing Piece was written in Schmargendorf.

Requiem, written in the diary "evening, 20 Nov. [1900]," was composed on the death of Gretel Kottmeyer, a friend of Clara Westhoff. Next day Rilke wrote Clara: "On the eve of your birthday you made me rich and wonderful with your letter about the wreath. Much moved by it I have written a big Requiem for Gretel, which I will copy for you someday when I have time.—You give me a great deal, Clara Westhoff." In the diary the poem is preceded by the following entry: "Clara W. writes today of a black ivy-wreath, and what she tells is again a whole poem. How she speaks of this heavy black wreath which she unsuspectingly fetched from the gable of her house out of the gray November air and which now in the room becomes so monstrously serious, a thing in itself, one thing more suddenly and a thing that seems to grow heavier all the time, as though drinking up all the grief that is in the air of the room and in the early dusk. And all that is then to lie upon the thin wood coffin of the poor girl who died there in the South; in the hands of the sun. The black wreath will press the coffin in perhaps, and its long tendrils will creep up the white shroud and grow in with the folded hands and grow in with the soft never-beloved hair, which, full of hardened blood, has also gone black and flat and will, in a dead girl's dusk, hardly be distinguishable from the leaf-hearts of the ivy. . . . And through the empty corridors of the blood the ivy will go, leaf after leaf, on its long tendrils, like nuns who lead one another by a rope and make pilgrimage to the heart that has died, whose doors are only leaning on the latch. I would like to write a Requiem with this picture."

NEW POEMS

THE first part of the *New Poems* appeared late in 1907, dedicated to Rilke's friends Karl and Elisabeth von der Heydt. The manuscript was practically ready for the printer by the end of June, but Rilke kept it another month "to observe it for a while in its continuity, which is still new to me." He shrank from inventing names for books of poetry and gratefully accepted the publisher's suggestion of the title, which allowed of a second part to follow, already in his mind. This appeared in 1908, with the brief but significant dedication, "*à mon grand ami Auguste Rodin.*"

The way Rilke deals with his subjects in these poems—subjects that include sculptures and paintings, many of which must unfortunately remain unidentified for the present—is witness enough to the widening of his experience during his close association with Rodin, his own consciousness of which Rilke often acknowledges in his letters. His awareness of his own advance is now further clarified for him by his experience of the work of another plastic artist, this time a painter. He writes to his wife, while looking over the first proofs of *Part I*, on October 13, 1907: "I notice by the way Cézanne keeps me busy now how very different I have grown. I am on the road to becoming a worker, on a long road perhaps and probably only at the first milestone." And a few days later (October 18th): "You must have known while you were writing, how much good that understanding would do me which involuntarily sprang from the comparison of the blue sheets [the ms. of both parts of the *New Poems*] with what I have come to know through Cézanne. What you now say and heartily confirm, I somehow suspected, even though I could not have indicated how far that development has already been realized in me which corresponds to the immense forward stride in the Cézanne paintings. I was only convinced that it is inner personal reasons that make me stand more seeingly before pictures which a while ago I would still perhaps have passed by with a momentary participation but without turning back to them more eagerly and expectantly. It isn't the painting at all that I study (because despite everything I remain uncertain in the face of pictures and learn with difficulty to distinguish good from less good ones and am always confusing early- with late-painted ones). It is the turn (*Wendung*) in this painting, which I recognized because I myself had just reached it in my work or at least had somehow come close to it, probably long since prepared for this one thing on which so much depends."

Looking back from a lonely and unproductive moment at Duino in

December 1911, Rilke wrote Lou Andreas-Salomé that he was thinking "with a kind of shame of my best Paris time, that of the New Poems, when I expected nothing and nobody and the whole world streamed towards me more and more only as task and I answered clear and sure and with pure achievement."

The *Panther,* one of Rilke's most popular poems, was written in Paris in 1903: he held it over for the later volume, undoubtedly because he felt that much in the *Book of Pictures* was not "of equal birth" with it. In writing to the Countess Manon zu Solms-Laubach (December 16, 1907), he says: "I am trying to follow, as uprightly as I can, the way of artistic truth, which is my way. It has already once led to the 'Panther' and to one thing and another that you have found good, and so you know that it is not entirely false, and also this: that I follow it in deepest sincerity (*mit dem ernstesten Herzen*)."

The Swan: (N.B. *ungeschaffen* = uncreated, by implication unfinished, awkward; in old So. German dialect = *ungestaltet* = deformed.)

The Last Evening bears the subtitle "belonging to Frau Nonna," who was Julie, Freifrau von Nordeck zu Rabenau. Rilke writes his wife (November 6, 1907) from Breslau, where he had read some of his poems: "I drove out early to find the old churchyard where Nonna's first young husband rests. In the still cold, through which a little sun was filtering, I found, amid sympathetically old-fashioned surroundings, the overgrown ivy-grave and read, before laying ivory-yellow roses down in the ivy, the simple tablet: Dodo Carl Georg Count Bethusy-Huc/Sec. Lieutenant in the Gards Rifle Battalion/b. Sept. 6 1835/volunteered 1 June 1866/fallen in the Battle of Königgrätz 3 July 1866. This, with everything round about, was like a new strophe to the 'Last Evening,' there already before the others."

The daguerreotype which is the subject of *Youthful Portrait of My Father* was confiscated with his other possessions when war broke out, Rilke having "without presentiment" left Paris for a journey on July 20, 1914. It was later returned to him, however, and is now in the Rilke Archive at Weimar. Joseph Rilke had died on March 14, 1906.

The Carousel was also a well-liked poem. At a reading in Prague which he describes in a letter of November 4, 1907, to his wife, "I read poems from the Book of Pictures, then Christine Brahe [from the *Journal*]. Then new things: Except for the Carousel nothing was even picked up. Everything lay where it fell. The program will be something like that everywhere." Two days later he reports from Breslau. where things went a little better, that "the Carousel again found its friends."

Song of the Sea (Capri, Piccola Marina): Rilke spent the months from December 1906 to May 1907 in Capri, where his friends the Faehndrichs put at his disposal a little "Rosenhäusl" in the grounds of the Villa Discopoli.

Archaic Torso of Apollo: (N.B. *unerhört* = unheard-of = fabulous = legendary. Of the possible meanings of *Sturz,* the brilliance or "plunge" seems to fit the action of the poem better than the static "lintel"; if the architectural concept seems nevertheless more justified it might be expressed here by "span.")

THE LIFE OF THE VIRGIN MARY

ON the afternoon of September 28, 1900, Heinrich Vogeler brought Rilke an old sketchbook in which two of the pictures—one an Annunciation to shepherds, one a scene "On the Flight"—caught his attention and inspired him to jot down several lines of verse in the diary next day. The subjects must have stayed by him, for in a manuscript-book he prepared for Vogeler that autumn were included the two poems *Annunciation over the Shepherds* and *Rest on the Flight into Egypt* now in *The Life of the Virgin Mary*. A plan to write a *Marienleben* to be illustrated by Vogeler never came to anything. But on January 6, 1912, Rilke writes his publisher from Duino that he is somewhat embarrassed by Vogeler having brought up the idea again; though their old friendship remains intact, he no longer feels that sympathy with Vogeler's work which would be necessary to such a collaboration. He asks for a copy of the two poems from the book, "for I have only the very vaguest recollection of them"; and he adds that for such a cycle several more poems would be needed "which Vogeler cannot have found among my things because so far as I know I have never made them." Vogeler's revived plan never materialized as such, but Rilke was inspired by the episode to write the cycle as it stands here. On January 24, 1912, he sent Lou Andreas-Salomé two poems (we are not told which) "copied from a quite new little Marienleben." In the same month he sent the manuscript of the whole cycle with a dedication to Frau Kippenberg. We may assume, then, that with the exception of the two earlier poems, *The Life of the Virgin Mary* was written at this time, probably at Duino, where he had been since early in December 1906. It was published in 1913. While he spoke of it later (January 22, 1920) as "a little bywork," he nevertheless had an affection for it. "It is a little book that was presented to me, quite above and beyond myself, by a peaceful generous spirit, and I shall always get on well with it, just as I did when I was writing it." (Rilke to Hugo Salus, June 28, 1913.)

CONTINENTAL LITERATURE IN NORTON LIBRARY AND LIVERIGHT PAPERBACK

NORTON CRITICAL EDITIONS